COMBATING
CHILD SEXUAL ABUSE

COMBATING CHILD SEXUAL ABUSE

An Advocate's Story
From Inside a Rape Crisis Center

By

MILLIE BONATI

This book tells the story of women pioneering the battle against child sexual abuse. The stories depicted are composites that have been compiled from hundreds of cases that happened over a twelve year period. The accompanying dialogues are amalgams drawn from over a thousand interviews during the same period. Names and identifying characteristics have been changed to protect the privacy of individuals. The intent is not to focus on any particular victim or abuser but rather to shed light on circumstances that can lead to abuse, what to do about it once it is alleged, and how to ensure justice for all.

© 2013 Millie Bonati

ISBN: 1479116637

ISBN 13: 978-1479116638

Library of Congress Control Number: 2013901718

CreateSpace Independent Publishing Platform, North Charleston, SC

In loving memory of Dick: May peace be your companion.

For Pam, Patti and Richard: You never let me forget that love matters the most.

I am especially grateful to the child sexual assault victims and their families who courageously shared their stories with me. You are the true pioneers who battered down those walls of secrecy. You made this book possible.

CONTENTS

Preface

In 1980, when my husband, Dick, and I built our dream house and retired to the pastoral countryside of New Hampshire, I envisioned a leisurely lifestyle. Instead, energized by a group of young feminists, I began volunteering for Rape and Assault Support Services of Nashua, New Hampshire (Rape and Assault). Much to my surprise, after completing their training program, I started covering a weekly shift on the crisis line supporting battered women and rape victims.

The first child sexual abuse calls started trickling in about a year later, catching the agency off guard. I heard sobbing, hysterical, terrified, confused, or angry voices in states of shock; professionals seeking advice; parents begging for help; victims crying out for support. Then came the inevitable plea, "Can you *please* talk to this child? I think she might have been sexually abused."

No one knew what to do. The criminal justice system at the time had yet to try a case with a child as the plaintiff. There were no protocols in place. Rape and Assault was soon flooded with calls. Although we were inexperienced and understaffed, *somebody* had to listen to these children. Under the supervision of our dynamic director, Deanna Crawford, I worked on my first cases, literal on-the-job training that soon led to my handling cases independently.

After five years as a volunteer, I joined the staff as their Child Sexual Abuse Coordinator, a position I held for seven years. In that capacity, I also became a spokesperson for the agency and fought for changes in a system ill-equipped to tackle an onslaught of children seeking justice.

Hundreds of cases later, my head is crammed full of stories. I have pretty much heard it all.

Child sexual abuse headlines continue to shock us even today. People often question me on the subject. It amazes me how little most understand about the nitty-gritty of child sexual abuse. The glaring absence of knowledge in this area prompted me to write this book.

My memoir takes the reader on a step-by-step journey that explains why the reporting of child sexual abuse exploded on the scene, seemingly out of nowhere. It sheds light on that burning question, "How could something that awful be kept secret for so long?" Riveting case studies are interspersed with behind-the-scene details of the methods our agency used to change the system. Readers get in on the ground floor and gain a behind the scenes, "in the trenches" comprehension of the issue.

Education is the key to winning the war on child sexual abuse. *Combating Child Sexual Abuse: An Advocate's Story From Inside a Rape Crisis Center* gives a horrific story meaning by bringing the issue to life with a rare, first-hand look at what's behind the headlines to show what remains to be done today. This account provides the knowledge to help us combat this sinister crime.

Millie Bonati

January, 2013

1 An Unlikely Volunteer

1980 was the year President Carter told a group of American athletes that the U.S. wouldn't be sending a team to the Olympics in Moscow.

It was the year that John Lennon was killed outside his New York City apartment.

It was the year that an interview by NBC's Tom Brokaw turned my world upside down.

Tom Brokaw's guest on the *TODAY* show was Deanna Crawford, the new Co-Director of Rape and Assault Support Services of Nashua, New Hampshire (Rape and Assault), a crisis center for battered women and rape victims founded in the 1970's by a group of local women who were inspired by the Women's Movement.

When Deanna became the co-director of the agency in the late 1970's, little was known about the widespread prevalence of domestic violence. Like most others, I thought that kind of thing happened to the poor, uneducated class, probably when the guy had too many beers and the gal did something to provoke it.

Even though Deanna worked out of an office only twelve miles from my home, the distance separating me from the feminist movement could have been measured in light years.

In 1948, I had packed my bags and headed for New York City after having graduated from the University of Connecticut with a BS in Marketing. After a tedious search, I beat the odds for my day and became a female member of the Manhattan male elite as a Marketer/Advertising Copy Writer for *Ronald Press Company,* a publisher of college textbooks.

Although I loved my stimulating, two-year career in the Big Apple, once I married my college sweetheart and moved to Connecticut, I found the long commute exhausting and I quit my job. Based on references supplied by my boss who was Vice President of Marketing at *Ronald Press Company*, I found a challenging position close by as a Market Research Analyst for *Marketing Research Company of America*.

Although my career was fulfilling, my top priority was to be a wife, mother, and homemaker, and I gladly quit working after the birth of my first child, rejoining the workforce as a teacher when my third child entered second grade. Because I was content with the free choices I had consistently made, in addition to getting along great with men, it never occurred to me that women *needed* liberating. If I could be liberated, why couldn't any other woman?

However, today, many factors have caused me to re-think that scenario. A recent contributor is the highly acclaimed TV Series, *Mad Men,* about the ruthlessly competitive world of Madison Avenue advertising. That show is historically accurate in the way it portrays the sexism of that era. The writers of that show are not sexist. The time period was. When I viewed it, it hit me how easily I had become a part of that male-dominated world. It made me reassess whether I might have had advantages other females of my era didn't. Advantages that made it easier for me to feel liberated.

In the 1950's, feminism wasn't a cultural option for most women. It wasn't until the 1960's that the National Organization for Women (NOW) gave many women the tools to fight discrimination. I recalled that when I hit Manhattan cold turkey, newspapers still ran separate ads with separate pay scales for female jobs. After weeks of having doors slammed in my face, I landed a newly-created, female executive job, one tailor-made to make me a member of their all-male marketing team. It never occurred to me that I wouldn't succeed, and I did succeed. That self-confidence never left me.

However, I also had my foot in the female world of that time in that I gladly gave up my career for my role as a homemaker, and I happily joined other homemakers in my attempts to play the expected role of a somewhat "perfect wife and mother."

Looking back, I can see that I had a foot in both worlds, unusual for that day. I loved both worlds. Each one strongly impacted the other. Perhaps, at times, they were also in conflict, each one demanding expression, exerting a greater influence on my life than I realized at the time.

However, all I was aware of on the morning of Tom Brokaw's interview with Deanna was that my eyes were glued to the TV screen as I marveled at her self-confidence while she educated millions of viewers about the harsh reality of battered women and how it crossed all walks of life.

The following day, I didn't understand the forces that prompted me to pick up the phone and call Deanna, but I did. A pleasant voice answered, "Rape and Assault Support Services. Deanna speaking." I introduced myself and said how impressed I was with her *TODAY* interview; how I had recently moved to New Hampshire; how I had read good things about Rape and Assault in our local newspaper; how I'd even mulled over the thought of volunteering but was afraid to work with violent people.

Deanna's simple answer had a profound impact. "Perhaps we can help you work through your fears." I had never considered that possibility. After a lengthy conversation, I remained apprehensive but said I would consider attending their upcoming Volunteer Orientation Class.

I was excited about having made the connection but my rebellious mind immediately rattled off a list of excuses as to why I shouldn't go. I knew nothing about counseling battered women or rape victims. I'd done my share of volunteering. The college bills were paid and, for the first time in twenty-five years, I wasn't employed and cherished my free time. I'd earned it. Why be bothered with other people's problems? Besides, I would never fit in with those aggressive women libbers I watched with disdain as they burned their bras on the nightly news. I was way too *feminine* to be one of them. I agreed with my husband, Dick, when he blasted them as unappealing, unfeminine man-haters.

In truth, I had paid scant attention to the Women's Liberation Movement. When it surfaced in the turbulent, drug-filled, Vietnam years of the 1960's, years that rocked America, I was consumed with raising three teenagers.

In my defense, I did listen to activists fighting for women's rights on *The Phil Donahue Show*, the first tabloid talk show that began in 1970 and went on to have a 26-year run on national TV. Day after day, I sat enthralled as Phil and the feminists uncovered the injustices that women were subjected to. Was I that out of touch with how many women and children were mistreated?

So it was with grave apprehension that I attended Rape and Assault's Orientation Class along with twenty other prospective volunteers. I used the back row as a good vantage point to look them over to see if they passed my critical eye. They didn't look like a bunch of radicals. I liked the way that most were dressed in the current fashion, with a touch of make-up—first impressions were important to me. Did they even want an elderly misfit to join them?

I was pleased that Deanna opened the meeting promptly. She welcomed us, introduced the staff and volunteers, and then had us introduce ourselves. When it was my turn, I had a hot flash and mumbled so softly, I doubted if anyone heard me. I was usually self-confident; why was I so nervous?

The staff members and volunteers presented different aspects of the agency. They were well-organized, knowledgeable, and passionate about their cause. I was practically knocked off my seat when I found out that Kathy Schoenley, their Co-Director, had even been a guest on *The Phil Donahue Show*. She was one of five women who gave themselves a title, met in each other's kitchens, and advocated for a woman's right to choose. Wow!

When the meeting ended, prospective volunteers were given a thick, three-ring binder crammed with information that would be covered over the next ten training sessions. Curious, I decided to take it home, look it over, and return it the following week.

As I drove home immersed in my thoughts, a strong, unfamiliar, inner voice demanded to be heard. "Those women remind me of the ones on *The Phil Donahue Show*. I didn't know that so many women and children were crime victims. Those Rape and Assault women are pioneers, righting a wrong. I want to be one of them!"

Even though it was well past my bedtime when I got home, I was too wound up to sleep. So I scooped out a big dish of praline ice cream, flopped on the couch, and opened the manual. In the silence of my living room, I became immersed in another world as I devoured well-researched articles on battered women and rape victims, along with what little information there was on child sexual abuse victims.

Thankfully, the next morning reason ruled. "I don't *want* to be associated with those victims. I've worked too hard to break loose from the pathos of my own family dynamics by making sure I became a winner. The last thing I want to do is jump back into that muck."

Regardless, I finished reading the manual and learned that Rape and Assault was a non-profit organization providing emotional support and information for victims of domestic violence and rape, through a 24-hour crisis line. They also offered a safe, confidential emergency shelter—a comfortable home in a residential environment, where advocates helped them rebuild their lives. Those gals were really something else.

When considering whether or not to become a volunteer, I felt overwhelmed by the magnitude of making such an involved commitment in an area where I had no expertise. Plus, I loved the freedom of my new life in New Hampshire and had lots of interests. Weighing everything, I decided to return the manual at the next meeting, then leave.

When I got there, my feet had a mind of their own and, once again, I slunk into a back row seat and listened to an in-depth presentation about battered women and Rape and Assault's supportive role. Each succeeding week, I found another excuse to go, always reassuring myself that I could leave at any time. This youthful group of activists continued to both fascinate and intimidate me.

One of the most shocking things I learned was how inept the authorities were in handling the sudden onslaught of battered women and rape victims who were coming forward. Authorities who should have protected the victims—police, county attorneys, judges, and members of the legal system—at the time all males—were caught off guard and unprepared. They weren't accustomed to having critical women peering over their shoulders.

When re-considering whether or not to become a volunteer, it was crucial to me that Rape and Assault worked outside The System. I was not cut out to be a social worker. What excited me was fighting to bring about changes in an ill-equipped, inequitable system. Being an independent agency, Rape and Assault was obligated to no one, so it could take on a watchdog approach and instigate a call for action. I liked the way they monitored how The System handled the cases; the way they fought for necessary changes; the way they raised public awareness; the way they spoke to the media whenever they saw an injustice; and the way they commanded respect when officials realized that their words and actions could be splattered in the local papers or aired on the nightly news.

During the training sessions, the Rape and Assault staff worked at making me more comfortable in the group, asking me easy questions to get me to open my mouth. When I sputtered that I wondered if I fit in with the feminists because I liked men, they smiled and said that the first misperception I had to lose was a generally held belief that all women libbers harbored resentment against men in general. I must admit it appealed to me that the staff and volunteers were mostly family oriented.

Midway through the training, I mustered the courage to move to the second row. When I interacted with the prospective volunteers, I admired how they made time for such an involved commitment when most had fulltime jobs and families that needed tending. They applauded my willingness to do something like that at fifty-three years old. Several said they wished their mothers would be more active instead of sitting home and complaining.

So, even though I had tried to convince myself otherwise, sink or swim, I knew I was hooked. The passion of those women libbers had won me over!

2 Life After Fifty

When I completed the training sessions with Rape and Assault, I had become much more enlightened about women's issues. I realized that the women's movement had left me in the dust, even though in the 1960's it had burst suddenly into the public consciousness and quickly grew into the largest social movement in the United States.

I learned that the movement developed in two separate streams. One was a structured national set of organizations, which coalesced around *NOW* and sought equality for women within mainstream institutions, such as government, employment, and labor unions. The other stream was informally named *Women's Liberation Movement*, made up of mostly young college graduates. This more radical stream concentrated on changing personal, social, and cultural life, and challenged the male-dominated power structure. It focused on issues that had not previously been considered political, such as housework, beauty, reproductive rights, violence, and sexuality.

Even though I could see where the increase in the number of cases of domestic violence and rape victims caught the male-dominated criminal justice system unprepared, I often empathized with their confusion; most weren't callous or uncaring—just uninformed, like most of us.

As the training period progressed, I worked hard to comprehend the issues, to become skilled in how to handle crisis intervention calls, to understand the dynamics behind dysfunctional and abusive behavior, and to become familiar with the area's resources.

I continued to be in awe of the women who ran the agency, especially Deanna. At thirty-eight years old, she was a glamorous wife and mother and a gifted, articulate speaker who stood up to the males in the Criminal Justice System and used the press to expose how ineptly New Hampshire handled cases of violence against women and children.

I wasn't aware of how unassertive I was until I hung around with those women. How could I not have fought for *Equal Rights for All (ERA)*? Why was *ERA* so fiercely debated when all women wanted were the same rights as men? My blood boiled when I thought of how long men dictated that women were too inferior to vote. Three cheers for the Women's Liberation Movement! The women activists, past and present, became my new heroines.

However, when the training ended and it was time to use what I had learned, my newfound confidence went poof. I wasn't ready to handle a crisis line. I must have been nuts to do this. When the staff felt a new volunteer was ready to cover the crisis line, she was signed up for a twelve-hour shift. Long after Deanna said I was ready, I kept saying that I needed more hands-on experience. "I'm so afraid I won't handle people in crisis well and will do major damage to them. It is a huge responsibility. I must be fully prepared. I'm not ready to risk a victim's welfare."

I sat in on many cases that Deanna handled, and marveled at her skills. She knew just what to say to each person. The victims placed such trust in her. She became my role model. "When I think about a victim getting me as an advocate instead of you, it just seems so wrong."

Deanna shook her head. "Millie, don't you think I was nervous when I started? We all have to get through that initial fear. You are as ready as the other volunteers who are manning the crisis line. If you're afraid you won't know the answer to a client's question, just say you don't know but will get back to her." In weekly meetings where the new volunteers shared the cases they had handled that week, I sat there like a timid mute, envying their confidence.

I averted their eyes when I was the only trainee left who hadn't signed up for the crisis line. I had to take the plunge or slink away in defeat. I puffed out my chest and said to Deanna, "Okay. I'm ready to sign on." Because most volunteers had daytime jobs, I signed up for the 6 a.m. to 6 p.m. week-day shift. Deanna assured me that she would be in the office all day for backup.

I tossed and turned the night before my shift started. My notebook and pen sat on my night table, right next to my bed, ready to take immediate notes. My clothes were laid out. My car keys and pocketbook were on the dining room table in case I got an early morning call to meet a victim at a hospital or police station. I was relieved when 6 a.m. finally arrived. I ate a filling breakfast for energy. 7 a.m., 8 a.m. No calls. I picked up the phone and checked for the dial tone. It was still there. When it rang about 9:30 a.m., I jolted to attention. "Okay Millie; it's time to face the music."

3 Sunday Morning Flowers

I cleared my throat and gave a couple good coughs before I picked up the phone to take my first crisis call.

"Hello."

"This is the answering service. I have a call from a Jackie whose husband threatened to kill her and she's scared." I took down Jackie's phone number and, with trembling hands, called her right back. A timid voice answered.

"Hello."

"Is Jackie there?"

"This is Jackie."

"Jackie, my name is Millie. I'm an advocate from Rape and Assault Support Services. How can I help you?"

Jackie's words rambled on in a heightened state of anxiety as I weighed every word carefully. "This morning, my husband put a knife to my throat when I said I was going to leave him. He's punched me before when he's had too many beers but he never used a knife before." Jackie's voice cracked. "I don't know what to do. I'm afraid to stay and afraid to leave. I'm scared to death he's going to kill me."

I swallowed hard. "It took courage for you to make this call. Where are you calling from? Are you safe?" I didn't hint that she was my first case. People in crisis need to feel that they are in strong, capable hands. I hoped I could fake it.

I asked Jackie to tell me more about the physical violence. She said, "It started with him slapping me around, and then punching me when he said 'I had a fresh mouth.' However, now he does it just when he gets mad or has a bad day. He's usually sorry the next day and says it won't happen again, but it does. One Sunday he even bought me flowers."

Jackie struggled to get the words out when she told me that he also forced her to have sex when he's drunk and she doesn't want it. She was shocked when I said that was rape.

"You mean it's rape when it's your own husband?"

"Yes, it most definitely is when it happens against your will."

"Wow."

When I had prepared myself to cover the crisis line, I was terrified that my mind would go blank, so I wrote step-by-step outlines of what to say to victims in crisis, covering every contingency I could think of. My notes covered such areas as active listening, supportive comments, questions to ask, and what resources were available.

I pulled out my sheet on Domestic Violence and told Jackie that she could apply for a Temporary Restraining Order (TRO) in District Court that would forbid her husband from having any further contact with her. I could meet her there and help her through the process. Once her husband was served with the Restraining Order, he would then have the right to request a Final Restraining Order Hearing, with both parties in attendance, within five days. I could also be there to provide support. At that time, a judge would hear both sides of the story and then decide if he would grant a Final Restraining Order.

About a half an hour and many tears later, Jackie decided to get a TRO. We agreed to meet in the back row of the courtroom. I would be wearing a light gray pants suit, with a royal blue turtleneck. I would have the necessary papers for her to fill out.

When I entered the District Court House for the first time, my knees shook. I may have looked professional in my sharp outfit, but I couldn't fool my pounding heart. Victims with glazed looks. Ill-at-ease people who had broken the law. Family or friends who listened intently. Attorneys explaining last minute procedures to their nervous clients. Everyone in their own little world. I sat down on a bench to absorb this foreign-looking scene and muster my courage to enter the courtroom. At last I got up, opened the big door, and took a seat in the back row.

Five, ten, fifteen minutes passed—no Jackie. Would my first case be a no-show? I watched a snuggling couple sitting in front of me. He had his arm around her, stroked her hair, and whispered softly in her ear. She smiled in response. He was probably offering her support for some court matter. They looked so nice in lieu of all the reading I had done lately on batterers. Then, she turned around as if looking for someone and saw me sitting there.

"Millie?"

"Jackie!?"

I later found out that Jackie's husband had talked her into telling him she was getting a Restraining Order and he was using his charm to get her to change her mind. I struggled to regain my composure. This wasn't covered in training. I gestured for Jackie to sit next to me. She and her husband had a tug of war, but because he probably didn't want to make a scene in the open courtroom, he let her go. Jackie jumped up quickly and sat beside me. Her husband and I locked eyes. His threatening glare terrified me. He looked as though he would like to use his knife on me. I knew I wasn't cut out for this. I envisioned tomorrow's headlines, *"Battered Woman and Advocate Stabbed Outside Courtroom."* How I wished I could turn the clock back and be in my comfortable, safe home that I loved so much.

Jackie and I ignored her husband. While we filled out the necessary forms, he stormed out. Jackie was shaking even more than I was. Fear was written all over her face. Suddenly, calm descended. I lost my fear when I realized that I had the skills to guide her. I might be inexperienced, but having me was better than her having nobody. She hung on to my every word just as I had seen clients do with Deanna.

When the judge called Jackie's name, we went up to the bench and handed him the papers. The judge loomed large as he peered over his glasses, asked who I was, read over the statement of why Jackie wanted a TRO, and asked about her current safety and financial status. Then he granted her a TRO, stating that her husband was to leave the house, give her temporary financial support, and have no contact with her until the Final Restraining Order Hearing.

With the TRO in hand, we each drove our own cars to the Police Department where a pleasant officer met us in the lobby. My voice sounded strange to my own ears as I introduced myself for the first time as an advocate for Rape and Assault Support Services. Then he spoke to Jackie in a gentle tone and asked her where she would like to have the Restraining Order served. She asked to have it done at his place of work so he would know he couldn't come home.

My pager suddenly beeped, breaking into the drama. Oh no. How could I handle two cases at once? Because of the call, I had no time to process the culmination of my first case or discuss Jackie's "freedom." We said an emotional good-bye in the parking lot; I told her to call the answering service if she needed to talk and I would call her back. She gave me an impulsive hug before heading for her car. Then I called the answering service from the nearest pay phone (no cell phones) and learned that there was a battered woman waiting for me at the hospital.

My second and last call that day resulted in my placing a battered woman, Alice, and her two young children, a boy and a girl, in our shelter. To this day, I am haunted by the frightened eyes of those two youngsters while their mom and I put fresh sheets and blankets on the beds. I choked back tears as I counseled the three of them, trying to allay their fears and prepare them for what lay ahead. I made arrangements to pick Alice up at the shelter the next morning and take her to the District Court where she would apply for a Temporary Restraining Order. Then I put them in the hands of Rita, our Shelter Manager. As I left, she was showing them where the food, toiletries, and racks of clothing were.

That night, I had phone calls from both Jackie and Alice who needed reassurance that they had done the right thing; they both remained fearful of their husbands. After that, I barely had the energy to change into my nightgown and crash into bed at 9 p.m. It took me a long time to drift off to sleep as I pondered the emotions of Jackie, Alice, and her kids as they faced the long, black night.

4 Second Thoughts

For the next several months, I covered the crisis line one day a week, gaining confidence with each case. Most calls involved domestic violence. I was sympathetic as I listened to the horrific stories and cringed at the sight of bruises and bloodied lips. I was especially surprised to learn about the damaging effects of verbal abuse, about how an insecure wife could be worn down when repeatedly told she was useless, ugly, dumb, controlling, demanding, or flirtatious—that her behavior was the reason the husband was so miserable. Many times, battered wives cried more over words than physical blows. One battered wife sobbed the most when describing how her husband said she had the face of a dumb cow.

Although each case was unique, there were common threads— the bruises, the low self-esteem, the vulnerable state of the victim, the fear of prosecuting their husbands, the fear of making it on their own, the scared eyes of the children, and the high incidence of alcoholism among the abusers.

However, as my caseload mounted, I started to become impatient and disheartened because many victims returned to their husbands. After a honeymoon reunion, they often called us once again for help. Some had a history of this back and forth behavior pattern. Had I wasted my energy on them? Couldn't they see they were setting themselves up to be victimized, that they were worth more than that? Didn't they hear me when I explained that abusers followed a pattern of coercive behavior used to attain power and control? That even though the violence may not happen often, it remains a terrorizing factor? That the violence usually escalates over time?

As time went on, I became increasingly disillusioned. I worried that I was spinning my wheels and wasn't cut out for this type of work. It took me a long time to realize that my arrogant expectations fed my frustrations. Who was I to judge how difficult it was for a wife to leave her husband, that it might take several attempts before she could make a final break? Or how much a woman with low self-esteem desperately wanted to believe her husband's tearful apology of how sorry he was and how "next time would be different." Or her paralyzing fear that she couldn't support herself and her kids when they were already so deep in debt?

Had I heretofore rationalized the existence of an unjust, patriarchal society? I had always maintained that Mother Nature meant for men to be the boss and gave them testosterone to make them more aggressive. Women were meant to be the nurturers. This arrangement was necessary for the survival of the species. I liked being a female, protected and cared for by my husband. Most of my friends felt the same way. It felt so right, so natural.

However, now a strange, retaliatory voice inside of me snapped back. "Although there is some truth in that, it doesn't give men the right to wield power over women, to deny them their rights, to treat them as second-class citizens, or to abuse them." I was beginning to understand on a gut level why the feminists fought so hard for their cause.

I researched the topic. I read books on women's struggle for equality, including parts of the Bible. I smiled when I viewed Jesus as a Women's Libber thinking that today he'd probably have a bumper sticker on his car proclaiming equal rights for women. I was appalled to learn about the injustices toward women throughout the ages. I felt the anger of all the women activists who went before me and I was indebted to them for the groundwork they had laid. I cautiously joined the rebellion against the stereotypical role of women. I became a pursuer of the truth, challenged to take a second, third, and fourth look at my entrenched beliefs.

This new understanding dredged up unwanted memories from my own past, one sprinkled with abusive husbands and submissive wives. I thought I had put all that aside by denying my family history and gravitating toward winners. No wimpy whiners for me. When I became a rebellious teenager, I had retaliated with silent, fiercely independent words, "That's not how my life is going to be. I'm going to be a winner, not a loser."

New insights appeared on the horizon. Even though I had forged a positive life for myself, I recognized that I had some unfinished business. Possibly, I was drawn to the feminists *because,* for the first time, they showed me a positive way to look at this issue that didn't tolerate wallowing in self-pity. Did the times I lived in give women choices that were unavailable to the trapped women in my family background?

While I was in this state of mind, I even wondered if I stood up for myself enough in my own marriage. This was scary territory because my marriage and family were my rock. I wondered whether I was denying a part of myself in order to create an image of a perfect marriage and home life—the accepted role for most "successful" women in my generation. Was I afraid to show the slightest crack in that unrealistic illusion?

Rape and Assault was the place for me during this period of inner upheaval. I was obviously ripe for a mid-life change. The staff had endless patience with my inexperience. They taught me the thrill of making a difference. Their fresh, radical outlook was inspiring for a neophyte like me. I just needed time to sort it all out and come to some new conclusions.

5 Rape: It's All About Power

After several months with Rape and Assault, I had yet to get a call from a rape victim. However, because the staff had weekly meetings with the volunteers to discuss all new cases which came to the agency, I got a first-hand education on the issue.

I was acutely aware that I was a babe in the woods when it came to understanding the dynamics behind rapes. I had bought into the many myths about why men raped such as: it was an impulsive, animalistic act fueled by strong sexual arousal; or women asked for it when they dressed and acted provocatively and then, when the men lost control, the women teasingly screamed, "N0. Stop it."

I learned that rapes are acts of violence—the assailant uses sex to inflict humiliation or exert power and control over the victim. Rapists can be anyone. Most are married or have ongoing relationships. The rapist is motivated by the need to dominate someone. In more than half of all reported rapes, the victim and rapist know each other. Child victims know their rapists in more than 80% of cases.

The details that spewed out of the mouths of rape victims who came to us were bone chilling to hear—the rage and strength of the offender, the heavy body squashed against the breasts, the strong hands strangling the neck, the knife pressed against the throat, the bone-breaking facial beatings, and the need for the rapist to be in complete control. Whether the rape happened recently or long ago, the victims exhibited similar trauma when they recounted it. The violent nature of the crime, along with the realistic fear of being maimed or killed, lingered long after the rape.

In the 1980's, there were no protocols in place to treat rape victims. Sandy Matheson, our Program Director, and Deanna worked tirelessly to implement mandatory procedures on a state level. Largely through their efforts, a Forensic Sexual Assault Medical Exam Kit is now available at New Hampshire's hospital emergency rooms. This kit mandates that every victim is thoroughly examined, with necessary medical and legal evidence collected. The hospital is then instructed to contact the crisis center as well as the police. The mandate does not require that the victim speak to either one unless it is something she chooses to do of her own free will.

At many hospitals today, the victim will be examined by a Sexual Assault Nurse Examiner (SANE), who is a Registered Nurse especially trained to provide comprehensive care to sexual assault survivors. The SANE nurse helps avoid further trauma, gives timely medical/forensic examinations with complete evidence collection, gives appropriate referral for follow-up care and counseling, and testifies in court when necessary. More than 50 New Hampshire Registered Nurses and Advanced Practitioners have completed the required training to become a SANE, and most New Hampshire hospitals now have a SANE on staff.

At Rape and Assault, advocates were trained to listen to a rape victim's story, counsel her, and then notify the police. They were the investigators; we are not. Even so, I always found myself weighing the evidence whenever I heard about these cases. The enormity of such an allegation could destroy someone's life. How would I fare if a female wanted revenge and falsely accused my husband or son of rape?

Sadly, we at Rape and Assault learned that a rare few did lie—an ex-wife who wanted her former husband and their friends to pity her; a teen-ager who wanted to get back at her ex-boyfriend and confessed when hooked up to a lie detector; a lonely widow who wailed that now she *had* to move in with her daughter's family. However, the checks and balances of a system that includes victim advocates, doctors, nurses, detectives, therapists, county attorneys, judges, and lie detector tests is near-impossible to fool—the above three "victims" eventually confessed.

Of all the advances in the last decades surrounding the arrest and prosecution of rapists, none have been more revolutionary than the testing of DNA. The genetic strands of DNA are unique to each individual and can link a suspect to a sex crime with cool scientific certainty—a tool more trustworthy than a witness's recollection or a host of other forensic measures.

Today, well-trained professionals handle rape cases in New Hampshire. As the public becomes more aware of why men rape, the myths that "she either asked for it or consented to it" are losing favor. Rape is a violent crime that leaves its mark on victims, victims who need counseling and support in order to begin the long healing process.

Because unforeseen events soon took me off the Crisis Line to assume other duties, I had minimal contact with adult rape victims. Even so, the gruesome details reported by other volunteers and staff members remain seared in my memory.

6 Capital Protest

As I continued to be exposed to man's darker side in my work, I gradually toughened my hide. Above all, I learned that victims needed someone who could hold it together while hearing horrific details.

At the same time, I often came home wiped out from the day's events, fuming with anger, or on the verge of tears. Dick became concerned about my emotional state. "Rape and Assault is taking over your life. I don't like this new you. You're turning into one of those woman libbers. It's a turn-off. The tail is wagging the dog." I was aware that we were not living the lifestyle Dick envisioned when we moved to the New Hampshire countryside. When we lived in Connecticut, most wives were full-time homemakers and social secretaries while the husbands were the main wage earners, roles we both enjoyed and never questioned.

In response to Dick's criticism, I was huffy and defensive. "I'm hitting a healthy balance. I'm keeping up with the housework. I've met other wives in town, joined the Women's Club, joined a dinner club, and nurtured some couple friendships I thought you'd enjoy. I enjoy being with our new friends." However, underneath, I knew the feminists had the stronger pull. The changes they represented were exciting.

One Monday morning, when Dick was leaving on a five-day business trip, I promised to pick and freeze his young, tender string beans in his prized garden while he was gone. I woke up Thursday morning planning to do just that. Then Deanna called to say that the staff was going to a Sentencing Hearing in one of the first child sexual abuse cases to be prosecuted. The hearing was to be held in Concord, our state capital. Would I like to join them? Hungry for the experience, I jumped at the chance. I'd pick Dick's beans that afternoon.

It was my first time in Superior Court and I was all eyes and ears as we walked briskly to the courtroom. I recognized the Defense Attorney of a highly publicized case where a wife was on trial for murdering her abusive husband, proclaiming self-defense. Reporters and TV cameras hovered around them. I had a fleeting thought that I would rather sit in on that case instead. It was headline news.

However, I followed our group into the courtroom as we took seats down front. Advocates from several women's crisis centers around the state whispered to each other in hushed tones, mostly about what an important Sentencing Hearing this was, how it would set a precedent.

The Hearing involved a twelve-year old girl who had disclosed an ongoing sexual relationship with an older family friend. Because prosecuting a child sexual abuse case was rare in the early 1980's, members of the media were present. Electricity was in the air.

When the judge entered in his impressive black robe, everyone stood up until he made himself comfortable in his big leather chair. Then we sat down on the hard benches. He gave a cursory look at the spectators in the courtroom, shuffled a few papers around, and got right to the crux of the case. Basing his ruling on technicalities, the offender was relieved of any guilt. Case dismissed.

Gasps filled the courtroom as the judge quickly gathered up his papers and left the bench. I didn't understand the mayhem that ensued. Disbelief. Indignation. Everyone talking at once. A demand for action. What was going on? Didn't they have to accept a judge's ruling?

When we left the courtroom, TV cameras zeroed in on us and reporters fired questions at the disbelieving advocates. I listened intently to their responses trying to understand what all the commotion was about. Surely judges must follow the New

Hampshire laws when they hand down a sentence. These women advocates may not have agreed with his interpretation of the law but he must have been within his legal rights.

I was star struck as I watched Deanna speak to the TV cameras. "The Judge blatantly said that consensual sex is okay with a twelve-year-old child. I beg to differ. In New Hampshire, sexual contact with a twelve-year-old is a felony." Was Deanna right? Was the judge's ruling against the law? Even though Deanna's rage came through, her nostrils flaring, she was composed and articulate; I was proud to be part of the agency she represented. I almost fainted when a member of the press wanted my views and I frantically pointed to the staff members who spoke for the agency.

The furious advocates made plans to meet at the State Coalition office to plan their next move. I fleetingly thought about Dick's string beans hanging on the vine. However, since I drove up with the staff, I was forced to be part of the action.

Indignation fueled the activists' cause. Within two hours, they had planned a protest march to be held in front of the State Capitol building the following morning. They drafted a statement that spoke for all the crisis centers, made protest signs, obtained a permit, and alerted the media.

As a novice and cautious by nature, I feared that maybe they hadn't done their homework. Was there a precedent ruling on a past case that could back up the judge's decision? I poured through their legal books but couldn't find one. Deanna teased me about my actions long afterwards. "There we were planning a major protest and there was Millie, sitting on the floor, reading books!"

They agreed on a time and place to meet the following morning. When Deanna assumed that I would surely want to go, I replied meekly. "Mmm—I promised Dick I would pick and freeze his string beans while he's away. Tomorrow's the last day I can do it."

The room grew deathly silent as everyone stared at me in disbelief. Someone finally found her voice. "At a time like this, you're thinking about *string beans?*"

At that moment, something in me changed forever. Gone was the guilt I had struggled with. I reset my priorities. Fighting for the rights of child sexual abuse victims was more important than string beans. I took a deep breath. "Of course I'll be there."

When I got home, I watched the coverage of the upcoming protest on the evening news and then read about it in the morning paper. I had never been involved in a news-breaking story. Women's voices can be heard! Deanna's voice resounded in my head, "If you're not part of the solution, you're part of the problem."

Early the next morning, I drove to Concord in my own car thinking I could still pick Dick's beans if I got home early enough. I parked my car and then joined a slew of media waiting on the capital steps for the protestors to come marching into view.

"Here they come! Look at how many there are."

I puffed out my chest as I watched them march toward the capital building with Deanna in the lead, her flowing skirt and black mane of hair blowing in the brisk summer breeze, holding a sign condemning the judge's decision and proclaiming that sexual relations with a twelve-year-old child was a felony.

The police cleared the road; the media snapped pictures and stuck microphones into the faces of the protestors. Cheering onlookers formed around the picketers, and faces peered out of every capital window. I hoped that cocky judge was watching.

Fired up, I joined the marchers, and grabbed a sign that said *Child Rape is a Crime*! I shouted protest slogans at the top of my lungs. What a thrill to protest for a cause I believed in! When a reporter approached me, I was so caught up in the passion of the moment that I lost my fear of talking to the press. Anything for the cause! With so much to say, it was vital that each voice be heard. I voiced my indignation into the reporter's tape recorder as she snapped my picture. Little did I know that she was from the Associated Press and that that picture would be carried over the wires throughout the country!

When we ended the protest, we collapsed on the capital steps, thrilled at the coverage. The public was outraged at the ruling and judges learned that they were going to be held accountable. From that day on, child sexual abuse in New Hampshire was a crime, punishable by law. As I drove home, I was psyched. Rape and Assault can use the power of the media to fight child sexual abuse. What a powerful weapon!

Standing in the hot July sun fired with emotion had wiped me out. When I shuffled toward the house, I gave Dick's beans a fleeting glance, made a beeline for the bathroom, filled the tub with hot water, slid in, and soaked my weary body. Flashbacks of the day seemed surreal. Conventional Millie protesting in front of the New Hampshire Capital building chanting "Child rape is a crime?!"

Dick's rich baritone voice startled me back to reality. "Hello. Is anybody home?"

I closed my eyes and groaned. What would he make of all this? Did he notice his unpicked beans? I yelled downstairs. "Hi. I'm in the tub. I'll be right down."

After hugs and kisses, Dick got right to the point. "I see you didn't get to pick the beans."

I blabbered incoherently. "Dick. You won't believe the week I had. I'm really sorry about the beans. I really meant to freeze them. But I just had to join a protest in Concord and…"

"Hold it. Did you just say you protested in our State Capital?"

I took a deep breath. "Yes."

Dead silence. Dick finally spoke. "I think we should pour ourselves a glass of wine, sit on the porch, and you can start at the beginning."

Once settled in, I told him what happened in great detail, so he would get the whole picture and see why I just had to do what I did. Dick showed little reaction. Why did I feel like a child who confessed something I did wrong, begging to be understood?

When I finished, Dick finally spoke. "You've had quite a week. We're both tired and I think we should talk about this some other time. What's for dinner?"

I always had a nice hot dinner ready when Dick came home from a trip. "I didn't have time to make anything. Is take-out pizza okay?"

Not a favorite of his for dinner, Dick grimaced. "It'll have to be."

In the days that followed, Dick brought the "subject" up in bits and pieces, usually to ask a question. Both of us were in unfamiliar territory. We sensed that I had changed the rules about what my expected role in our marriage was. This would take some getting used to, for both of us.

Others commented to Dick about my picture in the paper. "When did Millie turn into a Women's libber?" "What do you make of all this?"

Dick seemed ambivalent, vacillating between "You should feel proud of yourself", and "You're changing and I don't like the changes I see."

However, for me, there was no turning back. When the child sexual abuse cases soon started to trickle in, I found myself on a speeding train with a wide-open throttle and no brakes. The cause increasingly consumed me, as much as I protested to Dick that it hadn't. Once again, I tried to justify that I was hitting a healthy balance between my work and home. Because of Dick's own, legitimate needs, he didn't buy it.

In retrospect, what I hadn't fully admitted to myself at the time was that no matter what else I was doing, the cause dominated my thoughts. Deanna and the other dynamic women I worked with had me fired up. My passion empowered me with non-stop energy. Each little success emboldened me. At times, I occasionally wondered where that compulsion had come from. Was it all altruistic? I honestly didn't know. All I knew was that child sexual abuse was finally out of the closet and I was thrust right there on the ground floor; I had a powerful agency behind me and I was going to join the agency in combating it head-on.

7 It Doesn't Happen in Our Town

Child sexual abuse cases continued to be few and far between. To encourage victims to come forward, Rape and Assault opened a Child Sexual Abuse Crisis Line with a recorded tape giving them information and a phone number to call for help. Unfortunately, help in the community was almost non-existent. One chief of police didn't think there was a problem. "The need isn't there. This doesn't happen in our town."

One day, Deanna took a tearful call from a teenaged incest victim, Jamie, who lived in that police chief's town. Jamie had called our crisis line. Deanna made arrangements for the two of them to meet in Deanna's car. Deanna got permission to audiotape the meeting. Tearfully, Jamie described the sordid details of ongoing sexual abuse by her father.

After speaking with her for a couple of hours, Deanna assured Jamie that she would get help for her and made arrangements for Jamie to be in touch by telephone. After they parted, Deanna headed straight to the police station, stormed into the building and plunked the tape on the desk of the police chief. "Listen to this and then tell me it doesn't happen in your town."

When she returned to the office, she soon got an expected phone call. "It happens in our town. Bring the victim in."

Thus began Rape and Assault's first incest case.

When I volunteered for the agency in 1980, I covered a weekly, twelve-hour shift on our Crisis Line. While handling domestic violence cases, I gained invaluable experience working with people in crisis. However, when a rare child sexual abuse case came in, it was always referred to Deanna as the volunteers lacked the necessary experience to handle these delicate cases.

Because Rape and Assault operated on a shoestring budget, with only two full-time and one half-time employees, the steady rise in the number of battered women and rape victims had stretched them to the breaking point. The staff put in many unpaid hours.

When child sexual abuse cases began to trickle in, I could see the grave pressure this put on Deanna's time and I offered to help her in any way she saw fit. Since I was free during the day and she was desperate for relief, Deanna said she would call me when a child sexual abuse call came to the agency and I could sit in on it when she spoke with the child. From that day forward, Deanna took me under her wing; I could not have had a better teacher. She was inspiring to work with. As I gained experience, she let me handle aspects of the cases on my own and, ever so slowly, I learned how to handle a variety of cases in a sensitive and professional manner.

When she felt I was ready, she asked if I would volunteer to cover for her on days when she had to be out of the office. I readily agreed, both scared and excited to take this next step. It took a couple of months, but my first child sexual abuse case finally came.

8 Family's Best Friend

One night, ten-year-old Claudia lay wide-awake in her bed shivering. She climbed out of bed, slowly walked to her parent's bedroom and stood by the side of their bed. When her sobs woke them up, she blurted out the words she had practiced all day. "I don't want Mr. Reid babysitting us anymore."

Her parents shook themselves awake. They were dumbfounded to hear what their daughter had just said. Mr. Reid was a neighbor, the family's best friend, a bachelor who often babysat to give Penny and Frank a night out. He was going to babysit the children the next day when their parents were going to the stock car races.

Claudia wouldn't say why she didn't want him babysitting anymore. She just stood there with heightened shivering. She finally whispered, "I'm... I'm scared to tell you why because— you know that gun he shows Dad a lot?" The parents nodded their heads. Claudia hung her head. "Mr. Reid said he would shoot anyone who squealed about what he makes us do when he babysits."

"Claudia—what does he make you do? You've got to tell us everything. You don't have to be afraid."

Claudia blurted it out all at once. "We have to let him feel us under our clothes. Then he pulls out his pecker and makes us rub it. Sometimes he rubs it against us."

The parents were aghast. "Oh my God, Claudia—are you *serious*? Does—does he make everyone do it?"

Claudia nodded her head. "You can wake them up and ask them. They're just as scared as I am to be with him. We even talked about hiding when he was here until you got back."

The devastated parents frantically gathered up the other children and brought them to their bedroom—Leslie, 15 and John, 11. Sleepy-eyed, they woke up with a jolt when they realized their secret was out. Long into the night, the children told about the sordid things Mr. Reid made them do. The parents almost collapsed after their children confessed. They hugged their kids and told them it wasn't their fault as they all cried together. The kids were jubilant that their parents weren't mad at them for doing that dirty stuff, and because they never had to be alone with Mr. Reid again.

In her shell-shocked state, Penny kept shaking her head as she murmured in a shaky voice, "Where do we go from here?"

Early the following morning, I was nursing my first cup of coffee at home while leisurely waking up, when a call came in from our Answering Service. They had a message from a Penny, who identified herself as a mother whose three children had been sexually abused. Since Deanna was out of town, I was covering for her in the event of a child sexual abuse call.

Everything happened at such a machine-gun pace, I didn't have time to panic at the magnitude of the case. I acted on blind, gut-generated energy.

When I called Penny back, she spoke in a slow, deliberate manner as she described in great detail what the children had told her and her husband, Frank. She said she remembered reading about Rape and Assault in the newspaper. "Can you please help our family? We don't know what to do." I mustered up a voice full of bravado when I assured her that we were there for them.

When I said I would like to meet with the family, Penny said the children would be more comfortable if I came to their house. They were scared and that way she and their father could be there to support them. I took down their address and said I would be there within the hour. (This rule was soon changed and we were only allowed to meet clients at safe, designated places.)

As I drove to their house I thought about how Deanna might handle this case, remembering the cases of hers I had sat in on. I could almost hear her voice meeting the family, giving them confidence, praising their courage for coming forward, and then gently getting them to tell their stories. Deanna would have been confident that they *wanted* to tell their story and that it was our job to soften the entrance into a criminal justice system that was totally unprepared to handle children as victims. Digesting that information bolstered me. When I pulled into the driveway of their two-family house, exited the car, and gently knocked on their front door, I felt prepared. Penny opened the door as I was still knocking.

She led me into the kitchen where everyone was seated around the kitchen table. I barely squeezed into a tight space as everyone moved their chairs to make room for me. Her husband, Frank, looked haggard as though his mind was elsewhere, perhaps wondering how his best friend could have done this. The pajama-clad children stared at me, wide-eyed.

After we introduced ourselves, I thanked them for having trust in me during such a big crisis in their lives. I inhaled a deep breath and stayed calm so they would feel they were in safe hands. The skills Deanna had taught me were kicking in.

Penny immediately took charge and told the kids to tell me what they had told her and their father during the long night. And so began their long, sordid stories about what Mr. Reid made them do. They said his pressing his pecker against their butt was the worst, the most painful. They said they were terrified to say no to him because of that gun he threatened to use if anyone squealed. We spent the better part of the day getting the gruesome details from each child. After their initial hesitation, the children gradually became more at ease and even seemed relieved to be talking about it.

Penny was the spokesperson for the family. Frank continued to look shell-shocked as he looked to her whenever I asked a question. She spoke in a depressed monotone but was unbelievably clear-headed; she wanted to know the best way they should handle the situation. I was amazed at how well she could hold it together during such a traumatic crisis. I was having a problem squelching my emotions and I wasn't their mother. However, her controlled behavior did seem to have a calming effect on the kids.

I slowly explained how these cases were handled, giving out as little information as possible so as not to overwhelm them. Contacting the police would be our first step. I could do that for them. A detective would set up a time for them to come to the police department. He would then take down the children's allegations, one by one. If he felt the children's testimonies were credible, of which I had little doubt, that would set the legal wheels in motion. I assured them that I would be there for them during each step of the legal process, and that they could call me via the Answering Service whenever they had questions.

I became personally involved as the case progressed through The System—police arrest, grand jury indictment, preparing for trial. Penny remained a reservoir of inner strength as she maintained control of the situation on the home front. The kids welcomed my home visits and I learned a lot about their everyday lives.

Leslie, the fifteen-year-old, remained leery of the prosecution process. She didn't like the idea of other people, especially her peers, maybe finding out about what happened to them. "Can't we just have nothin' more to do with Mr. Reid and let it go at that?"

When I opened up a discussion on the pros and cons of continuing to go forward, everyone had an opinion: "I hate him. I want him to go to jail for what he did." "He would do this to other kids if we don't stop him." "It *would* be a big relief to have it over and done with." "Other kids wouldn't find out about the dirty things we did if we just kept it secret among us." The final consensus was that everyone but Leslie was for prosecution. By this time, rage toward Mr. Reid fueled their actions.

After several months, Mr. Reid continued to plead not guilty so the case went to trial. Because there were numerous delays, a tactic used by defense attorneys to wear down children and families, I gave hours of support to the family as they struggled through this tedious procedure. Later on, when the number of child sexual abuse cases exploded, I would not have that luxury. In future cases, my main focus had to be getting the victims and families through their initial crisis state, steering them into the criminal justice system, finding the right therapist, and offering them limited support as I juggled several cases at once.

Before the case came to trial, Mr. Reid pled guilty and settled for a lessened jail sentence. I was greatly relieved as I felt this was in the best interests of the family. They were more than ready to put this nightmare behind them and move on with their lives. More than anything, the children were happy they could "thumb their nose at Mr. Reid and let him know we paid him back for what he done to us."

I often wondered if I would have had the guts to do what this family did. Their lives were disrupted for nearly a year. Their steadfast honesty and determination to do the right thing remains with me to this day. This was the first of many cases that would shake up my comfortable lifestyle and help reset my priorities.

9 Let Him Rot in Jail

Deanna began to feel comfortable with the way I handled child sexual abuse cases on my own. Although my inexperience gave me butterflies, I found child sexual abuse cases more challenging—we broke ground with each one. Because those calls were still few in number, I continued to cover the crisis line one day a week.

One morning, I was at the County Attorney's Office to discuss a case where the child had initially disclosed the sexual abuse to me. It was the first time an advocate from Rape and Assault had met with a prosecutor to discuss a case, so we were each feeling our ground. It turned out to be a warm, productive meeting, in the best interests of the child.

When our consultation was over, the young county attorney, prosecutor X, hesitated, as though pondering something. He finally said, "I have another child sexual abuse case I am preparing for a Grand Jury, my first such case. It involves four sisters, ages fifteen to nineteen, who have accused their father of ongoing sexual abuse. Could you possibly talk to the girls to see if you could elicit more information that could result in my handing down further indictments? They're coming in with their mother after lunch to prepare for the Grand Jury."

When I offered to read the file, prosecutor X brought me to a private room, handed me a thick folder, and asked if he could buy me lunch. I requested a tuna fish salad sandwich and "the biggest cup of coffee you can carry." After he delivered the meal, I settled in, sipped my coffee, and opened the folder. Although the abuse started when the girls were in grammar school, prosecutor X was only filing charges for what had occurred during the past five years, in order to stay within the current Statute of Limitations.

The report described the mother as a battered woman who was fully aware of the sexual abuse. I gasped. As an overprotective mother, I screamed inside, "How could a mother stand by and watch a father sexually penetrate their daughters for years and do nothing about it?"

My stomach lurched as I read the disgusting details. It was the heaviest case I had been privy to in my short tenure working with child sexual abuse victims. How could I not show my revulsion when I spoke with the girls? However, I knew they would clam up if I did, so I had to be in control of my emotions.

When I finished reading the file, I sat in the stillness of the room, trying to absorb what I had just read. Then I collected myself and discussed the case with prosecutor X. As bad as it was, he felt there might be even more charges. I told him I wanted to speak to the mother first so I could get a read on where she was coming from and ascertain what kind of support the girls could expect from her.

I was sitting in the silence of that stark room not knowing what to expect when prosecutor X ushered in a plain-looking woman with stringy hair pinned back with bobby pins, with missing front teeth. After introducing us, he left, and I started out by thanking her for agreeing to speak with me. She didn't appear ill-at-ease, shy, or embarrassed. She stared at me with a defensive glare. I went on to say how I had read the girls' painful testimony, the harsh facts, and asked how the girls were doing in light of all that had happened to them.

Given the severity of the case, she answered in a deadened, matter-of-fact manner, as she described how they were "gettin' on with it." That suddenly changed when I asked how she felt about the severe abuse her daughters had been subjected to.

She blurted out that she was as much a victim as her daughters. "I did the best I could've. There was nobody to talk to about it in those days—NOBODY. He had all the money so I couldn't of moved out. He had two guns locked up and said he would've killed all of us if anyone squealed. He showed us the guns with the bullets in them, and then pressed one gun against each of our heads and put his finger against the trigger and showed us how easy it would be to blow our brains out. And he would've did it too. I ain't kiddin'—I saved my girls' lives by puttin' up with the abuse."

I struggled to process this new information. I felt less judgmental than I did at the start. Her story curdled my blood. With a controlled display of emotion, I thanked her for her information and asked her to wait in an outside room while I spoke with her daughters.

Prosecutor X brought in the girls, introduced us, and quickly left. When the four sisters walked into the room, there was no hint of the ordeal they had lived through. With curious looks on their faces, they sized me up. Their shabby clothes were typical styles of their age group. They looked clean; their hair looked freshly shampooed. I had expected a downtrodden foursome to walk through the door but these girls seemed psyched. The fury and hatred they had for their father dripped like venom when they spoke. "Let him rot in jail for the rest of his life."

Eager to have their day in court, the sisters couldn't wait to testify. They were blood-thirsty. They wanted revenge. The sordid details gushed out as they repeated what they had already told the prosecutor: sexual penetration since grammar school.

As we spoke, it was as though the five of us were caught in some kind of hypnotic spell as I made the transition into their sordid, evil world. Strength from some unknown source enabled me to tolerate hearing the horrific abuse a father had subjected upon his daughters. After I "calmly" listened, I told them that the more details they disclosed, the more counts prosecutor X could hand down. "Did anything else happen that you didn't tell him?"

They looked at each other with questioning expressions as though they were deciding what to say. The second oldest daughter spoke up. "Let's tell her." They nodded their heads. For the first time, a look of shame spread over their faces. Then they all started to speak at once. Words gushed out. In soft tones, they described animalistic acts beyond horrific.

"He made us do it in front of each other." "He slapped the one he was doing it to if we tried to close our eyes." "He tied us all together, then looped it around the bedroom bureau so we couldn't run away." "When he did it up our cunt, at least he wore a rubber so we wouldn't have another brat for him to feed." "He liked it up the ass best of all." "Yea. That's the one that hurt the most." "I was so afraid he would kill us all if I told anybody what was going on."

It was almost more than I could bear to hear. My emotions turned to ice to keep me from yelling out in anguish. I couldn't believe a father would commit such vile acts against his own daughters. His sneering words to justify his actions were bone chilling: "All of you sit on your fucking asses all week while I work my ass off. This is my right." I wanted to cry and embrace them but I just listened in total silence.

When they were finished describing the abuse, their voices rose. "We were too embarrassed to tell those things to prosecutor X because his face got red when he asked us questions. It's easier talking to you because you're a lady and you don't act embarrassed."

When I finished writing down the new allegations that I could hand to prosecutor X, my eyes teared when I said, "I am so sad that this happened to you." For the first time, pain filled their eyes as they blinked back tears.

I liked all four girls, admired their courage, and emphasized how much good they could do with their lives because of what they had survived. Their tender feelings toward their mother were genuine; they truly believed she had saved their lives by putting up with the abuse. "He would've killed us if she told anyone. If he found out what she did to help us behind his back, she could've been beaten bad." I said nothing to shake their belief. A voice inside me said I would have done everything to protect my girls but I had no idea what it was like to have all your spirit beaten out of you by a sadistic father and husband.

My amazement intensified at how outgoing and animated they were, but as they spoke, I realized all their pent up rage had them fired up because the time had finally arrived when they could bring their father to justice. They would need that energized anger to get them through the emotional ordeal of the trial.

I asked what gave them the courage to speak out now. The youngest one answered. "When my sisters left home, I couldn't take it no more—being alone with him. Then I saw a show on TV that talked about it. Then someone came to our high school and talked about it. She said we should report any bad touching by a grown-up. After that, I walked to Miss Hayes' office—she's our guidance counselor—and just stood there cryin'. She jumped up, shut the door and told me to sit down. She was so kind and that made me cry harder."

"I told her about some of the things my father done—but not the real bad stuff because I was afraid she would think I was dirty and disgustin'. Then a policeman came to school to talk to me. His eyes got watery when I told him what I told Miss Hayes. He said he would protect me, that I don't have to be afraid no more. Then he took me to the police station and called my sisters and mom to come in."

The older ones chimed in. "We were all so glad it were finally out. We were at the police station a long time. The policeman asked lots of questions when he speaked to us one at a time; he typed pages of stuff while we talked. When we was finished, the police wouldn't let us go home until they arrested him. A judge fixed it so he couldn't pay bail and get out of going to jail. We felt so safe knowing he couldn't come after us. When we went home, we laughed and cried for the rest of the night."

"After the police arrested him, he got a lawyer and pleaded not guilty. We went to the Court Hearing just so we could get a look at him in court and knowed that we put him there. He looked like a shitty bunch of bones sittin' there. I couldn't get over how small and scared he looked. This coward held us in fear for our lives all those years? Now it was his turn to look scared. The fucking bastard—he weren't so brave once the police got hold of him."

The girls said they wanted to tell their story. They weren't ashamed of what happened to them; they knew it wasn't their fault. They wanted everyone to know that these things happened to people out there. Those victims should speak up and get help. They told me I could tell anyone. They *wanted* me to. They had kept it secret for so long when they were children and now that they were adults, they didn't have to keep it secret anymore. I told them I would tell their story without any personal identification.

As I ended our interview and slowly reentered the outside world, I thanked the girls for trusting me with their disclosures. I stressed that their new allegations were going to make it a stronger case. I told them how much I admired their strength and courage, that they had an important story to tell and were going to make strong witnesses. That they would send a strong message to fathers that they could get caught and sent to jail.

When I presented the new evidence to prosecutor X, he added several more counts to the upcoming indictment. He thanked me profusely and said he could see the important role Rape and Assault could play in bringing these cases to justice.

As I wound down my long day, I trudged to my car. Driving home, I digested the reality that the graphic details I heard today were real. Beyond horrific. If I continued to work on these cases, I knew I had to assimilate the evil that man was capable of doing while still maintaining my belief that most humans were innately good.

When I suddenly realized the impact of this case, blood surged through my veins. The County Attorney's Office and Rape and Assault had forged a mutual respect for each other's roles. These cases demanded the joint efforts of all the professionals involved, and I savored the fact that one more step had been taken toward confronting and doing something about the sordid reality of child sexual abuse.

I never saw the four sisters again. Prosecutor X told me later that the father received a five-year jail sentence. It would take time and further action before stiffer jail sentences were enacted.

10 Daddy's Special Girl

Child sexual abuse issues continued to get sporadic coverage in the media and Rape and Assault began to get a few more calls. I was now Deanna's back-up whenever I was free to do so. One day, Julie called me at home and referred a case to me.

When I returned the call and I identified myself, a deep baritone voice on the other end of the line spoke with a sense of urgency. "Thanks for calling back so quickly. I'm Reverend James. I have a problem and am not sure whom to call."

"Why don't you tell me what your problem is."

"A nine-year-old just disclosed to me that her father takes her to the movies every Friday night because he says she's "Daddy's special girl." But she doesn't want to go any more because she doesn't like the stuff that happens afterwards. When I asked her what kind of stuff, she said he touches her but she didn't want to say anymore. She just wanted me to tell her mom not to make her go with her daddy anymore. She said her mom would listen to me. I asked her if we could ask her mom to come in so we could talk about this together. She shouted back. 'NO. I don't want her to know why I don't wanna go with him.' "

Reverend James heaved a sigh that sounded as though he was out of air. "A whole bunch of questions ran through my head. Should I try and find out what kind of touching he does? Where do I begin? Then I remembered something Rape and Assault sent me in the mail about you speaking to children when they want certain touching stopped. Is this the kind of case you handle?"

"Yes it is."

"God Bless you. I did ask Sue if she would speak to a lady who helps children who want certain touching stopped. Sue said she would if the lady didn't tell her mom what she said. And that's when I called you."

"I'm glad you called. Sue trusts you if she confided in you; she definitely feels you are the safest way to reach her mom. I've interviewed other children who cry out for help in this way. If you can persuade the mother to bring Sue to our office, I could talk to her and try to find out what's going on. If it is anything sexual, it's common for a child to be terrified to tell her mom, especially if a father is the perpetrator. The mother's reaction is often a child's biggest fear."

Reverend James digested what I said and sighed once again. "That sounds like a good way to go. I will explain to Sue and her mother—her name is Dina—who you are and why it would be helpful for them to talk with you."

"Call me if they agree to come, and we can set up a time for us to meet."

"Thank you so much. God Bless you."

"Thank *you* for calling. You did the right thing."

After setting up an appointment, Sue and Dina arrived at our office, looking as though they were on the verge of collapse. Dina's eyes looked vacant, almost as though she wasn't there. Sue clung onto her rigid mother, her eyes brimming with tears.

I introduced myself and asked Sue if I could speak with her mom first. She nodded her head and I had her wait where the staff could keep her company.

Dina and I went into a private room. She sat on the edge of her seat and played with her fingers. She had yet to look me in the eye. I thanked her for bringing Sue in. "That tells me that you are a caring mom." I explained who I was, what my role was, and that I was experienced in talking with children who are afraid to tell their mom something. I said I wanted to speak with her first because a mother's reaction to what a child discloses is crucial. I told her I was going to try and get Sue to talk about why she didn't want to go to the movies with her Daddy any more, which was all Dina knew at the time.

Dina, like most mothers, had that shell-shocked look that mothers often had when they found themselves in a rape crisis center, daughters in tow. However, she listened intently when I explained that an honest show of emotion was okay—tears and sorrow for whatever Sue might have gone through, but that she must try to put Sue's feelings over her own and do what's best for her. "It's vital for Sue to feel she has your love and support."

Dina was glassy-eyed when she raised her head. "I'll do my best."

"I'm sure you will."

Then I brought Sue into the room and shut the door. We sat on straight back chairs facing each other. She looked like an all-American youngster with her trim figure, pug nose, freckles, and ponytail. Even though she looked scared, she looked me in the eye, a good sign. Many sexually abused children hide their heads in shame as though they think I am able to read their minds and knew the dirty things they had done. An important part of my job was to explain to those children that they did nothing wrong—that someone else did something wrong to them.

I opened the conversation. "Thank you for coming in to talk with me. It's scary to talk with someone like me who you don't even know, about something you don't want to talk about, and you have no idea what I'm going to ask. It took a lot of courage for you to walk through that door. Thank you again."

"You're welcome."

I engaged Sue in conversation about herself—her family, school, and friends. She was responsive, another good sign. That told me she was reachable. Not like some kids who are too terrified to say anything this early on. She had strong positives going for her—a fairly stable family, friends, good student, soccer team, and a church youth group.

I told Sue who I was and that I did this work because I care very much about children who are caught in a bad situation they're too scared to talk about. I offered to answer any questions she might have. Her first question was revealing. "Will anything I say to you get in the newspaper?"

"That's a question I get a lot. Kids are afraid of people finding out about what happened, especially their friends. The child's name is never put in the newspaper. Sometimes, the name of the person who did something wrong is put in the paper. Sue, you just told me about a fear you have. Every child I talk to has fears about telling bad secrets. What do you think some of those fears might be?"

By putting it in a third person dialogue, the chances were that Sue would address her own fears. She quickly replied. "The kid might be afraid that she will be taken away from her family."

"Lots of children say that. Why do you think a child would have such a fear?"

"Maybe she's been told she'd never see her family again."

"That's a terrifying thought. However, that rarely happens. Everyone works hard to keep a child in her own home."

"Is that *really* true?"

"Sue, I give you my word that I will always tell you the truth. I will never lie to you."

Sue stared at me for a long time, as though she was debating the truth of what I said. This was a critical point. Sexually abused children have usually been lied to on the deepest level and it's difficult for them to trust anyone. Once a child believes that I will answer the most difficult questions truthfully, we reach a level of trust that paves the way for honest communication. I continued. "Can you think of another fear a child might have about telling?"

"That maybe her mom won't love her anymore."

"That's certainly one of the worst things that could happen to a child. However, a mother's love is very strong—something like a mother bear who will do anything to protect her cubs. Because your mom brought you here, that tells me she cares about what happens to you. Do you think that's so?"

A faint smile formed on Sue's lips. "Yeah. My grandma always tells me that my mom loves me more than anybody, that she'd do anything for me, that she spoils me too much."

"Do you think your mom is something like that mother bear?"

Sue nodded her head.

We continued to address "other children's" fears. Sue was beginning to relax more and played less with her ponytail. She asked good questions; I gave forthright answers. I continued. "I have talked to many children who were afraid to talk about a bad secret. Sometimes, it helps if they first talk about the good and bad things that might happen if a child tells someone their secret. Is it okay with you if we talk about that?"

Sue nodded her head but looked apprehensive. I broke the ice.

"I thought of one. A good thing is that the bad touching would stop."

"But a bad thing is that my mom and daddy might break up and it would be my fault."

I noticed that she answered in the first person. I reinforced it in a calm manner. "A good thing is that you and your mom and daddy could be shown why it wasn't your fault; I could explain to them why bad touching is never a child's fault."

"A good thing is that I wouldn't have to go on special times with my daddy anymore."

"That's a biggie. However, a bad thing is that it is going to be very hard right after you tell because your mom and daddy may be very upset. Sue, do you feel that children who have bad secrets should tell?"

Sue took a long time to answer. She twisted her ponytail. "Yes. Because, if she doesn't tell, that bad stuff will keep on happening until she's old enough to move out of the house."

"You're right about that. You're a smart girl. Also, if she doesn't tell, the bad stuff usually gets worse. You'd have to wait about nine years before you would be old enough to move out."

Sue stayed quiet for a long time and I gave her time to process all this information. When she raised her head and looked up at me, I continued. "Have you had bad stuff done to you that you haven't told anybody about?"

Sue lost eye contact once more and hung her head. She looked close to tears. "What will happen to my daddy if I tell you about it?"

"First we would have to tell your mom. Depending on what your daddy did, I might call some people whose job it is to protect children. Then your mom and I would take you there to talk to them. What happens to your daddy after that depends on your daddy—whether or not he admits he did what you said he did or says you are lying. I could give you a better answer if you tell me what your daddy did during your special time."

Sue hung her head. Her voice was barely audible. "At first he just rubbed my privates with his finger."

"How did that feel?"

Sue's face froze; a look of terror crossed her face. She lost eye contact, hung her head, and spoke in a whisper. "I was scared but it felt good."

Admitting that it felt good is one of the most terrifying things a sexually abused child can confess. It makes them feel guilty that they liked this dirty thing that was being done to them; it fills them with shame and confusion.

"Sue, our bodies respond to certain types of touching; it's just the way our bodies are made. Lots of times that can be a good thing. Just because it felt good doesn't mean that you wanted it to happen. It's very wrong for an adult to do that to a child. Lots of children say it felt good. It's never a child's fault that it felt good."

Sue raised her head and stared at me. It was a powerful connection. She didn't say anything. She didn't have to. Relief was written all over her face.

"What happened after that?"

"He made me promise that I wouldn't tell anybody, that I would get him in lots of trouble if I did, that Mommy wouldn't love me anymore if she found out."

Tears trickled down her cheeks. I gave her a tissue, leaned closer and held her hands. "Sue—it's okay to feel sad and scared. You are brave to talk about it. I can help you so that this doesn't happen to you anymore. The more I know, the more I can help you. Is there anything else you would like me to know?"

Sue kept her head down as she spoke. "Last Friday, he did some more stuff."

"What kind of stuff?"

"He took his thing out of his pants and he made me rub it."

"What happened after that?"

"I started to cry and he held me in his arms, and said he loved me and that this was our special time together, that I was Daddy's special girl. He said he would never hurt me, that it would always feel good. That lots of little girls do this with their daddies to show that they love them. But if I told anyone, they would take me away from my family forever."

Sue's eyes were glued to mine when she finished. I spoke in a gentle tone. "Thank you for telling me what happened. I am very sad that your daddy did those things to you. He was very wrong to make you do that. I can see now why you were so afraid to tell. Your daddy lied to you when he said that lots of little girls do this with their daddies and that you would be taken away from your family forever if you told anyone. However, I'm happy you told me because it means that you never have to go on a special time with your daddy again."

Sue spoke in a whisper. "What will happen to my daddy?"

"What would you like to see happen to him?"

"I don't want anything bad to happen to him. He's a good daddy. He works hard to feed us and pay for the house. He reads me a story at bedtime. Once I was sick and he stayed up all night taking care of me. I just wanna go back to the way things used to be."

"You are very kind. Are you mad at your daddy for doing what he did?"

"No. He didn't mean to hurt me."

"Sue, your daddy did something wrong, and he may have to be punished. He has a problem and needs help. There are people who can help your family—kind detectives and social workers—I will take you to talk to them. After that, a lot depends on whether your daddy admits that what you said is true, that it was his fault and he needs help. Because you were brave enough to tell me your story, you can help him get the help he needs."

Sue sat there motionless. She gave a big, openmouthed yawn. I continued. "How do you feel now that you have told me what happens when you and your daddy go for your special time?"

"I'm scared about what Mommy and Daddy will say when they find out."

"I can understand why. That will be hard. Hopefully, I'll be there to help you through it."

"Good."

"Would it be okay with you if I stepped out for a few moments?"

"Yes."

As mandated by law, I called the Chief-of-Police in the town where the abuse happened and reported the facts of the case. He said he would contact a social worker and that I should bring Sue and her mom to the police station.

I quickly returned to Sue who stared at me wide-eyed. "What's going to happen now?"

"I'd like to bring your mom in and let her know what happened. Do you understand why she has to know?"

Sue closed her eyes. "Yes."

"This will be hard. Would you like to tell her, have me tell her, or have us tell her together?"

"I want you to tell her. I don't want to be in the room when you tell her."

"Okay. Should we go out and get her now?"

"Yes."

"Before we do, I want to say that you have shown a lot of courage today for a nine-year-old. What you have to face today is going to be hard. But you did the right thing. You should feel good about yourself for telling what happened so it can be stopped and your daddy can get the help he needs."

Sue and I went to get her mom. The long wait had taken a further toll on Dina. Her face looked frozen in fear and she avoided looking at Sue. She said nothing. I said that Sue asked me to speak to her alone and then I took Sue to our front office.

Dina walked like a zombie when I asked her to come with me. When we entered the room and shut the door, Dina sat down and stared at me in silence. I initiated the conversation. "Sue is a lovely girl. You are a very important part of her life. She loves you and her daddy very much."

Dina just stared into space. There is no easy way to break such devastating news to a mother. I spoke as gently as I could.

"However, there is a family problem that must be addressed." Then I told her what Sue had told me.

Dina let out a blood-curdling shriek. "I knew it. I just knew it. Why did she have to tell Reverend James and you? Why couldn't she have told me? We could have stopped their special time and we wouldn't be in this mess we're in now."

There was no stopping Dina's hysterical outburst. She was out of control.

"Boy—she's made some mess of my life now. Who's going to take care of us when they take my husband away? Can you answer me that? I don't want to do anything about this. I'm going to take Sue home and handle it myself."

My mind was on overload with thoughts of what I should do next. My heart was pounding but I kept my voice calm. "I'm afraid that's not possible. Because this involves alleged sexual abuse of a minor, I was mandated to report it to the Police. Dina..."

Dina screamed out, "You've already reported it? You had no right to do that without checking with me first. I just want to get out of here."

"Dina, please try to keep your voice down so Sue doesn't hear what you're saying. Remember we talked about how important your first reaction is. Once Sue told Reverend James she wanted her daddy's bad touching to stop, it was a case that had to be reported to the authorities. I can understand how devastating this news is for you to hear but there is help out there for you and your family. If you wish, I can be there to help you and Sue get through it."

Dina gave me a chilling, defiant look. "That's easy for you to say. Are you going to pick up the pieces of my life and put them back together?"

My heart ached for Dina but I had to act fast. "The police chief and a social worker are waiting for us at the police station. Sue will ride with me. We'll meet you there."

I quickly left the room and grabbed Sue by the arm. "Let's go. Your mom will follow us in her car." I grabbed our coats and rushed Sue to the car without looking back. I locked the doors and looked in the rear view mirror. I couldn't believe Dina wasn't running after us. She was nowhere in sight. I gunned the car and sped out of the parking lot.

After we drove for awhile, I pulled into a quiet parking area and spoke with Sue. "Like we had talked about, Sue, it was very hard for your mom to hear what had happened to you. She knows that we are heading to the police station now and she is going to meet us there. When she calms down, I'll try to help her understand why children don't tell right away, why they are so afraid to tell their moms. Why it is good that you told. I will explain to her how your daddy needs help and I will offer to help both of you get through this."

Sue nodded her head; she looked very sad. I hugged her and she clung onto me and started to cry. After she had calmed down, I asked her if she was okay for me to drive on. She nodded her head.

As I drove along, Sue asked if she could put on the radio; I let her choose the music station she wanted. This space gave us both time to collect our thoughts. I wondered where Dina was. Did I break the law by whisking Sue away from her mother? I had no legal authority to do that but I didn't want her mother's reaction to do any more damage. There was no easy way to do this. I had to get Sue in the hands of the authorities.

When we arrived at the police station, Chief Hall and Joan, the social worker from DCYS, were waiting for us. Joan immediately said that since this case involved a minor, the law mandated that she and Chief Hall interview Sue alone. I mentioned that other police departments allowed me to sit in on a child's interview to give the child added support, that she could check out my credentials. However, Joan held her ground. "That's not our policy."

Sue looked terrified when I said she had to go in the room with Detective Hall and Joan. I said I would wait right outside the door to be there when her mom arrived.

When Dina arrived at the station, she avoided my eyes, took a seat, and sat in silence. I knew from what Sue had told me that she was a caring mom. I could only imagine the pain and state of shock she must be in to know that her world had suddenly crumbled beneath her. I spoke first. "Sue is talking with Chief Hall and a social worker from DCYS named Joan. How are you doing?" Dina kept her head down and stared at the floor in silence. I respected her privacy.

About an hour later, Chief Hall and Joan emerged. I got a quick peek at Sue waiting in the room when they opened the door. I wanted to go in to her so badly and see how she was, but Joan got right to the point when she addressed me. "We appreciate your reporting the case to us. We'll take over from here. Confidentiality in cases involving minors mandates that we don't discuss it with you any further."

Chief Hall deferred to the legal authority of DCYS. Joan said she would explain to Sue and Dina why they would be taking over the case. I asked if I could say good-bye to Sue but Joan felt that, given the state of Sue's emotions, that would not be in her best interests. I didn't argue the point because other social workers had been upset when we had interviewed a child instead of calling them, even though we always guided them into The System. Knowing they had the law on their side, I thought it was in Sue's best interest not to create any further tension.

I could only watch as Chief Hall, Joan, and Dina went into the room and shut the door in my face. My heart was heavy. I hoped Sue didn't think I had just dumped her and didn't care what happened to her. From here on in, it was Dina's call as to whether or not I would ever see Sue again. I slogged back to my car.

Once I was safely home, the day's emotional impact hit me with a thud. Because I had never encountered a DCYS social worker before when I brought a child to a police station, I had never been so abruptly cut off from a child who had just entrusted me with her story, and it left me with an empty ache inside. I vowed to try harder to build bridges with DCYS so that this didn't happen to another child. Somehow, there had to be a gentler transition into The System for the child. But, it remained a sticky situation as long as each agency believed so strongly in its mission.

I never heard what happened to Sue and Dina.

11   Incest: The Father as the Offender

As I handled more father/daughter incest cases, they had me struggling with a dilemma. On one hand, they were the vilest of cases, demanding the worse punishment. However, this was not what most incest victims wanted, even though there were some exceptions such as in the chapter, *Let Him Rot in Jail* that involved the four sisters. Most incest victims wanted the abuse stopped, to have the father admit his guilt and then get help. Only in rare cases did they want their fathers taken away or jailed. However, how could I justify mercy for the worst crime and jail time for others? Researching the subject and writing the following paper helped me resolve this conflict.

FATHER/DAUGHTER INCEST

THE FATHER AS THE OFFENDER

Father/Daughter Incest. Close your eyes and try to visualize it happening to a father and daughter you know. It's a picture most of us can't tolerate. Outrage and disgust obliterate it. Words take over—"Scum." "Castration's too good." "Throw the bastard in jail for life." The father who commits incest—the most despised offender. Is there any punishment bad enough?

Yet, how little we know about him. What type of man sexually abuses his own daughter, leaving her psychologically scarred for life?

An average composite would show a man thirty years old, with average social intelligence, little psychiatric history, and no prior criminal record. He is immature, dependent, passive, rigid, selfish, and egocentric. He feels entitled to whatever he wants and doesn't understand what it costs others to provide it. He feels inept, abandoned by his own parents, and unable to express feelings. He is bored and disenchanted with life. He has a steady work history but feels stalemated in his job. His family is socially isolated, with poor communication skills. He is monogamous but he and his wife are drifting apart. His wife no longer seems proud of him. Sex with her has lost its spark and is used only to relieve tension. He fantasizes about sex with other females but doesn't have the skill or courage to follow through.

His favorite child, an eight-year-old daughter, is always there, cuddly, warm, and soft. He is flattered and stimulated by her attention. He slowly starts to caress her for warmth and comfort. He is surprised to feel the excitement of forbidden sex-play he felt in his childhood. Guilt and self-disgust make him stop. But the urge is too strong and he presses his sexual advances on her. Alcohol often lowers his defenses. He uses no physical force; his authority as a parent gets her to comply. He gradually increases his sexual demands.

Because father/daughter incest is so reprehensible, we perceive him as a depraved monster. The composite shows this is not usually true. He is an emotionally troubled person and his offense is more the product of immaturity. Otherwise, he leads a competent, law-abiding life. But we cannot isolate and observe him apart from his complex, human past. We must look at where, when, and how he became an adult, parent, and lover.

He was probably a victim in his formative years of physical and psychological abuse, neglect, abandonment, or exploitation, making him unable to relate to others. He probably had little emotional nurturing from his own parents and doesn't know how to give it. He represses his feelings, cannot express emotions, has few friendships, and is afraid to be himself. He feels angry, inadequate, hostile, helpless, insecure, isolated, frustrated, and powerless.

He has been conditioned by society to believe that his needs should be met by women and is angered that his wife no longer fulfills his sexual and emotional needs. He cannot understand not being cared for, nurtured, loved, and respected by a woman. "Women are supposed to do this." His misidentified emotions confuse his need for love and intimacy with sex; sex is the only intimacy he knows.

He has had few examples of tender, loving males in his life, so he emulates the only male he knows—the one that's strong, sexually virile, and authoritarian with his children. When this fails, he turns to the power of his genitals—his weapon. They will assure him of his competence and power and fill his need for "love." He uses them to act out his frustration on the least threatening person—his daughter.

This sexual act can be powerfully rewarding to him. He can structure the sexual encounter exactly to his liking with no fear that his performance will be judged or ridiculed. His excitement is heightened by the need for secrecy and sense of indulgence in the forbidden. The sexual act becomes an addiction—he enjoys it too much to stop; he crosses over that vague borderline between loving sensuality and abusive sexuality.

He does not see the pathology of his situation. Unable to lead a self-fulfilling life, he stews in chronic resentment, committing hostile acts subconsciously intended to be self-punishing. His self-abusive behavior is an unconscious reaction to his inner turmoil.

At times, his daughter's unhappiness over the incest can contribute to his enjoyment. The incest experience expresses his hostility to all women. He chooses his daughter to fulfill these hostile and aggressive wishes because she is the least likely to retaliate. Power may be the primary motivation. Consequently, he does not use his daughter primarily for sexual gratification, but as a means to confirm his low self-worth. He is unaware of the needs, drives, and motives behind his behavior or of the consequences to his daughter, family, and himself.

Other men have similar backgrounds and impulses and don't act them out. What makes him do it?

He has two characteristics common to incestuous fathers:

Lack of impulse control

This can be characteristic of him or it can be brought about by transient stress.

Confusion of roles

His daughter becomes something else in his mind—a surrogate wife, an object to fill his needs. He does not recognize the inadequacy of his daughter to fill these needs. He feels his wife and children exist only to serve his needs and he sees nothing wrong with his actions.

How does he get away with it?

He succeeds by committing the ultimate betrayal of trust.

He takes advantage of his daughter's innocence. She has been taught to respect and obey adults. In her eyes, he is the most special man in the world—she adores him. "Daddy wouldn't do anything to hurt me." He doesn't have to intimidate her—she openly trusts him. She is too young to know an incest taboo exists.

His seduction begins subtly. At first, his caresses feel strange but pleasurable. Their "special" secret meetings are exciting. "What Daddy says must be okay." She enjoys the new attention. It could be her first sign of being loved in the family. She doesn't perceive herself as being a sexual person. This new intimacy feels privileged, attention getting, warm, and loving.

As his sexual demands increase, she gets confused. He uses cajolery, trickery, threats, and bribes. "This is sex education," "A proof of love." "A daughter's duty," "A fun game," "All Daddies and daughters do it," "Don't tell or you're in trouble," "It's our secret," "I have a present for my special girl." It's a situation for which she is unprepared. She's unclear whether or not it is wrong. She doesn't want to cause him any trouble.

His growing demands increase her confusion. She is now unable to distinguish between parental love and his sexual behavior toward her. It is not her place to refuse her father. She lacks the experience or information to understand his sexual arousal. Trusting acceptance and curiosity are her role as she waits for him to define the limits of this new game.

When she questions him about what he's doing, he is deaf to her protests; parental possessiveness and sexual arousal have overpowered his protective role. He has suddenly put on a strange mask of love and she never knows what role he will play.

Her secret is now experienced as paralyzing fear—fear of punishment by her father, mother, school, or police if she tells; fear of repercussions to family; fear of her father going to jail and no one supporting the family; fear that no one will believe her; fear that no one will love her anymore—her family is her whole life. It's best if she just shuts up.

It takes years for her to realize that something is terribly wrong. "Daddy told me he was teaching me the facts of life." When she realizes the wrongness of the intimacy, she feels guilty and responsible. Confused, humiliated, in a state of disbelief, she feels helpless to stop it; sadly, she feels no one will believe her, or care if they do. So she continues to accept the only expression of closeness and attention she receives. Having no way to deal with her fears and anxieties, she sentences herself to a prison of abuse from which she sees no escape.

And there's the most painful fear of all. Can she survive admitting to herself that her own father used her to commit the ultimate betrayal of trust? Words of adult survivors express this denial:

"I didn't commit suicide. I have a feeling it was because there were good times too. Emotions are so hard, so funny to deal with. You can have one strong emotion one way and just keep it that way—like hate. But then something stirs up other memories. And he could be so good. And then so awful. And the pillar of the community. It's kind of funny, isn't it? He was just one mass of contradictions."

"But surely at fourteen, I should have been capable of escaping his oral sex, of preventing that. Of screaming perhaps? Or, as one psychiatrist put it, of "biting." Damn right. And I would have too, you bet, if I hadn't so carefully preserved a portion of my kid-self, wrapped nicely in tissue paper. That portion which held as tightly to a belief in the magical powers of fathers as to a stuffed animal."

What about him? Does he ever feel guilty? Is he pained for what he has done to his daughter? How does he handle disclosure?

From start to finish, he will deny most of what he's done. He will try to soften our hearts by telling us that he is innocent. In order to preserve his wavering self-image, and prevent having to pay the consequences, he will place the guilt and responsibility outside himself and his control. Under pressure, he will admit he did it but will deny any responsibility and claim he is the true victim. He will probably use part or all of three primary excuses common to incestuous fathers:

LOLITA: THE CHILD SEDUCER

He will blame the dangerous desires of little girls and how they're always getting men in such trouble.

"She was always walking around half-naked, wiggling her behind, so I did something about it."

"She's a regular little Brooke Shields, how she dresses. Little girls grow up fast today. They're just like women. They all want it."

THE WICKED WITCH: THE EVIL MOTHER

"Mothers are supposed to save the family from all problems, including incest."

"My wife was always nagging and bitching at me. She wouldn't give me sex. But my daughter looked up to me. She made me feel like a man. So I went to her for everything."

"My wife made me do it. It was her fault."

SANTA CLAUS: THE GENEROUS FATHER

"I gave my daughter what she liked and what she asked for."

"It wasn't like I was hurting someone. I was giving her the attention I thought she needed."

"I was trying to teach her about sex. I didn't want her learning it from some dirty-minded boy down the street. I wanted it to be gentle and caring for her."

"I loved her. She wasn't a happy kid. I wanted to help her. I should have picked her up and given her a hug. Instead, I put my penis between her legs. I just didn't know any other way to show my love."

Will therapy help him see that he is the guilty one?

His therapist will more than likely first see him as a non-threatening man, both charmer and wimp, acting out of distorted love or misplaced affection. If the therapist is comfortable with his own sexuality and can press him to accept responsibility, he will finally bring out what's beneath the surface.

"I confronted him with accepting responsibility for his actions. Suddenly, there was a tightening of his muscles, a clenching of teeth, a pounding of fists, a display that said, 'No masculinity is lacking here.' I sat there amid his rising anger, a grown man, and was afraid. Everything felt silent inside me. I could only think about his daughter facing him alone. The fear she must feel. The bottomless anger she must know is there, even when he is using her body politely, speaking gentle encouragements to her. Even when he is opening his need like a beggar, she must sense that her father is still her master and she must either obey or risk his rage. I could only think about how she had to find a way to survive this assault by herself--so totally alone."

Is there any way to right his wrong?

We must look at resources that help rather than destroy him. This can be hard to accept—the image of an eight-year-old daughter performing oral sex on her father evokes a revulsion in us that demands punishment. But we are not considering his daughter's best interests if we destroy him. Her overwhelming fear is that she has placed him and her family in serious jeopardy. We must not force her to bear this responsibility—it would crush her. We must replace our hateful reactions with productive interventions, by treating the complex psychological dynamics that led to his abusive acts.

98% of incestuous fathers will not repeat the crime once it has come to the attention of the criminal justice system and is dealt with. So, a treatment program within the criminal justice system that makes it safe for incestuous families to come forward is required, a structured program that includes all the officially responsible members of the community—police, social workers, mental health workers, probation officers, defense and prosecuting attorneys, judges, and rehabilitation officers.

Humanistic programs, modeled on this concept, have proven the most successful and least expensive in rehabilitating and reuniting the incestuous family. Most importantly, the psychological scars from his abuse are so deep that his daughter's chance of living a positive life is small without this sensitive and skilled type of treatment.

The enormity of the changes required for his rehabilitation cannot be overstated. He is not only asked to renounce a compulsive, pleasurable habit but also to give up power over his family and to become more responsive to the needs of others.

The words of an incest offender in treatment address this:

"The first step is saying, 'Yes. I did it.' But that's only the first step. The second step is tearing yourself apart and rebuilding. You have to go all the way down to the core. Every little nook and cranny that something is hidden in has to be pulled out. Every bit of it. None of it can stay down there. You can't say, 'This is my sexual part. I can just deal with that.' No way. It's the whole being that has to be ripped apart and rebuilt again, leaving a big empty void inside. An emptiness that used to be filled with something I didn't like. But I like what I am putting back in. I'm finding something to put back in that's fresh."

Father/Daughter Incest—the ultimate betrayal of trust.

The incestuous father forced me to confront myself with uncomfortable questions: Is there a limit to the power of forgiveness? Should incestuous fathers be given preferential, deferred sentences? But, whatever answers I come up with, I must remember that my views have to be subjected to the needs of the victims. They must be given their options and they, alone, must decide the path that is right for them.

12   Incest Diversion Program

Once I realized that incestuous fathers were rarely a risk to other children and that most incest victims didn't want their fathers prosecuted, I believed that the victims' wishes should prevail.

Based on my research, in order to achieve this goal, it would be necessary to implement an incest diversion program under the auspices of the County Attorney's Office working as a team that would include the Division of Children and Youth Services, police departments, judges, therapists, and child advocates.

Under the auspices of such a program, the father would be offered a deferred sentence in lieu of going to jail. In most cases, only the threat of a jail sentence hanging over his head had enough clout to force reluctant fathers to admit their guilt and enter family therapy. This therapeutic approach had the best chance of bringing incestuous families forward and stopping the abuse, the primary goal.

Unbeknownst to me, many years before I joined the agency, Deanna had maximized her efforts to get such an incest diversion program in place in our county. After months of preparatory work and numerous meetings with the various departments involved, it had been on the verge of being adopted. Then, at the last minute, a major player backed out. Since the program wouldn't work without that agency's full cooperation, the incest diversion program was shot down on the eve of its inception.

So when I enthusiastically showed Deanna information on similar programs that had been successfully adopted in other states, she opened the bottom drawer of her desk and brought out a copy of the failed program. She shook her head sadly. "I can't believe I have resurrected this proposal. The pain was so bad when it was defeated that I thought I could never look at it again."

Surprised, I took her proposal back to my desk and slowly read it. It was terrific—it entailed everything I had hoped for. My respect for Deanna deepened. "You were a visionary, ahead of your time." My enthusiasm for giving it another try gave Deanna renewed energy to pursue the project once again. I researched successful programs implemented by the more progressive states. I met with members of the Incest Diversion Team in Jefferson County, Colorado who gave generously of their time as they explained their protocols to me in depth, starting with videotaping the child's initial disclosure.

I mailed copies of Colorado's mandated procedures to our County Attorney in advance of a meeting with Deanna and me to discuss the possibility of mandating such a coordinated program, beginning with the initial videotape of a child's testimony. However, despite our best efforts, those in authority didn't share our views. As State Attorney General Stephen Merrill would explain to us later, County Attorneys are elected officials. They didn't want to appear to be soft on crime, keeping the option to throw the book at those "bastard fathers." New Hampshire was just not ready.

One of my biggest disappointments when I left Rape and Assault was the failure to get the first Incest Diversion Program adopted in New Hampshire.

13 Interviewing Child Sexual Abuse Victims

After I had handled several child-sexual abuse cases on my own, Deanna decided that I could best serve the agency as a volunteer child advocate on call rather than covering the crisis line. I welcomed this change because I was most passionate about the groundbreaking area of child sexual abuse. Now those cases would be forwarded to me at home, and I accepted the restrictions this put on my free time. However, I also set limits: When I was traveling, Deanna would handle the child sexual abuse calls. This arrangement worked out well for both of us.

Deanna and I became pacesetters in the field. We were in a unique position to spot the myriad of flaws in how The System handled these cases. We identified the changes needed to accommodate children thrown into a judicial system devised for adults. A child didn't stand a chance against an aggressive defense attorney with an arsenal of legal weapons.

In the beginning, many in The System viewed Rape and Assault as an adversary, infringing on their territory. They didn't like whistle blowers who used the media to point fingers. As Attorney General Merrill later told us, one County Attorney said he was terrified of us—one bad headline could kill his reelection.

The Division of Children and Youth Services (DCYS) claimed that every case of suspected child abuse should be reported to them, not Rape and Assault. However, we found that most adults who became privy to child sexual abuse allegations were hesitant to call the police or DCYS until they were positive that sexual abuse *had* occurred. They wanted a professional to talk to the child first, in order to find out what exactly happened and then guide them into The System. We filled that need.

The victims and their families became my teachers. Their courage to come forward with their heart-wrenching stories educated me about the complex dynamics behind child sexual abuse. As word got around that children opened up to me, I found that parents, relatives, therapists, nurses, physicians, clergymen, and teachers, among others, asked me to talk to children when they suspected abuse.

No one was more amazed than I that children put their trust in me and overcame the terror of telling their worst secrets. An unknown source gave me the strength and skills to help children in this way. When a child and I walked into a private room, closed the door behind us, and sat on straight chairs facing each other, deep dark secrets came out. Over time, I developed a heightened sense of what it took to gain a child's trust. This led to a flexible interview guide that helped a child to feel safe enough to tell me her story.

At the risk of being somewhat redundant, I will set forth a loose outline of how I interviewed a possible sexually abused child.

THE INTERVIEW

The interview would begin when the child was first brought to me, usually by her mother whom I spoke with first. I emphasized how vital her reaction was should her child disclose sexual abuse, how the lack of a mother's loving support could be more damaging than the sexual abuse itself. At this point, a mother's eyes often took on a glazed look as though she sensed that something horrendous was about to turn her world upside down.

After talking with the mother, I led the frightened child into the private room. My first task was to quell her initial fears of talking to me. I explained who I was and that I did this work because I cared about children who needed help. I thanked her for the courage it took for her to come into this room with me. I said that she could ask me any questions, at any time, as that would be helpful.

I then asked her easy questions about her life so she could get used to talking through her fears. Who were the members of her family? Did she have a pet? Did she like school? Who's her favorite friend? As she answered my questions, I assessed her strengths and weaknesses. What did she have going for her? Against her? How strong was her support system?

Each child came in with her own unique set of fears. It was vital that I addressed, validated, and defused her fears upfront. I often approached this in the third person as this was less threatening, using such words as, "Lots of children tell me they are afraid to tell me their secret because they're afraid of what will happen if they do. What are some of the reasons you think those children were so afraid to tell?"

Chances are a child's answers were based on her own fears. I then lessened those fears—"I can help your parents understand it was not your fault." "Everyone works hard to keep a child with her family." "The one who did the bad touching is sent away." "Losing your family's love is a BIG fear that seldom happens." "The one who did the bad touching is the dirty one." "Everyone feels sorry for the child." "A child's name is never put in a newspaper." I stressed that it was never a child's fault if an adult did something to her that was wrong; it was always the adult's fault. We would then discuss the pros and cons of a child telling vs. not telling secrets she might be keeping inside.

Once her fears were lessened, the child's age, maturity, and allegations determined the next step. I reassured her that I could be with her every step of the way for ongoing support, that I would help her tell her parents what happened, a child's major fear. It was all about making a child feel safe enough to tell me her story. Hopefully, I had now earned the child's trust and she knew she had a friend who was going to stay by her side. She would then begin to disclose what had happened to her, in a way that was right for her.

Whenever a child alleged sexual abuse, I was mandated, by law, to report it to either the police or to DCYS. They, in turn, had to report it to each other. If a parent chose to contact the police first, I explained to the child why this step was necessary. I reassured her that the detective was a friend, someone who protects children; that he would be dressed in street clothes; that he would ask questions similar to mine; that he would think she was very brave to tell her story; and that he would type up a police report as she answered his questions.

I would then privately call and identify myself to the detective on duty and give him the background information on the case. The detective would usually ask me to bring the child to the police station and then to sit in on the interview to lend the child support. Understandably, most children were terrified to go to the police station and talk about their dirty secret. They often gripped my hand in the parking lot as we approached the door. The detective would usually meet us in the waiting room and, after introductions, he would lead us into a private room.

In the beginning, most of my cases were a detective's first case of alleged child sexual abuse. Because, at that time, the detectives were all male and the victim and I were often the first females they had discussed sex with on such an intimate basis on the job, I kept a calm exterior and maintained eye contact while they got used to the situation. Most said afterwards that the child's testimony was a life-altering experience, that they were consumed with rage and wanted to nail the alleged perpetrator.

I was a life-raft for the child until she got to know and trust the detective. Every detective I worked with was gentle and tried to put the child at ease. They struggled with the uncomfortable situation of talking to a child about intimate sexual details, but never lost their professionalism. It took a long time to draw out the details of a child's statement as she was full of shame about the dirty things she did.

If a child looked to me for help, I squeezed her hand gently, told her she was doing really well and nodded for her to continue.

The child usually hung her head and spoke in a whisper when describing the abuse. Victims often said that their hearts were pounding hard and they felt dirty and ashamed because they were sure the detective would be disgusted with them once he pictured her doing those things.

It is crucial that a detective elicit as much information as possible in order to build a strong case. He needs explicit details of the sexual acts, with exact times and dates. I rarely interfered with a detective's interview. If I felt I had to, it was usually because I knew from interviewing the child earlier that she had left out a critical piece of information. I would usually just say a few carefully chosen words to nudge her memory.

There was stillness in the room when a child disclosed the abuse, a silence invaded only by the clickety-clack of the typewriter keys. I was often mesmerized by how fast detectives typed using the hunt and peck system, as their index fingers flew over the keyboard.

We made sure each child would have many breaks to stretch and move around. Unfailingly, detectives would bring her a soda or snack from the machine or even share their own, packed sandwiches. Thankfully, police officers love donuts and one or two often provided me with much needed energy to get through missed meals, as the hours dragged on.

Eliciting a police statement from a young child, on top of an already exhausting interview with me earlier, was draining for the child. Lots of yawns. I was consistently faced with the grave need to have the child's initial interview videotaped, with other involved professionals watching behind a one-way mirror, in order to spare the child the grueling task of repeating her story over and over.

At the conclusion of the police interview, I accompanied a weary child and adult (usually the mother who had waited in the waiting room) to their car. Children often told me that they slept the clock around once they got home. When I reached home, I usually collapsed on my couch and vegged out. I couldn't get the child's face, with all her many emotions, out of my mind. What else could The System do to make this barbarous procedure less intimidating for a young child?

Meanwhile, back at the police station, the detective would begin his criminal investigation to ascertain whether or not there was enough evidence to make an arrest. If he felt a child's imminent welfare might be endangered, he would immediately contact DCYS so they could instigate a Child Protective Investigation. They were mandated to report every case to DCYS within a certain time frame.

After a child gave her police testimony, many parents assumed that the police immediately arrested the alleged perpetrator. I would explain that the detective had to complete an investigation first and then weigh the evidence. Parents often thought it was incredible that a perpetrator who sexually abused their child was free to roam around until the wheels of justice did their thing. In those cases where the alleged perpetrator lived at home (father, relative), he would usually be removed from the home to insure the child's safety. Foster care was used as a last resort.

If a detective gathered enough evidence to make an arrest, the case would be sent to the County Attorney's Office. They, in turn, interviewed the child once again, examined all the evidence, and then determined whether or not to begin prosecution proceedings.

When the number of child sexual abuse cases increased dramatically, Rape and Assault no longer had the manpower to spend hours in Superior Court as victims weaved their way through the Criminal Justice System. Therefore, we lobbied for a Victim/Witness Assistance Program within the County Attorney's Office, one that would support the victim and her family throughout the long judicial process. Deanna and I had several meetings with the County Attorney and his staff to develop and implement such a program. Because we respected each other's roles, the transition went smoothly. Under the dedicated leadership of Director Catherine McNaughton and her staff, this program brought relief for the overworked county attorneys, produced stronger witnesses, and became an invaluable resource in the prosecution of child sexual abuse cases.

As my case load increased, I became aware of many common denominators, while remaining cognizant that each case had unique needs. I didn't succumb to burnout because it energized me to know that these crimes were being exposed, that victims were speaking out, and that changes were taking place within The System to ease their trauma.

14   A Ten Minute Break

On an early, rainy Monday morning a staff member called me at home to inform me that they had a possible child sexual abuse case. "The one who reported it is a school principal."

When I dialed the number of the school, the principal answered on the first ring and I identified myself, "My name is Millie. I am a child advocate for Rape and Assault Support Services. How can I help you?"

The principal's voice had a sense of heightened urgency. "A third grader just told her teacher she was raped this weekend. The teacher brought the student, Terri, to the nurse's office and then she came to my office. I immediately called in our guidance counselor. None of us knew what to do."

"Then our counselor remembered a conversation she had had with a colleague at another school who had faced a similar situation and called Rape and Assault. An advocate came to their school and got the child to tell her story. Can you help us?" she pleaded.

I reassured her that we were experienced in this type of situation, and told her I could leave within the hour. My voice was calm but my guts were churning. Deanna had only gone to a couple of schools to interview a child and I hadn't gone to any. This morning, Deanna was at a legislative meeting and I was on my own. It was crucial that I gave the school and the child the help they needed. Rape and Assault's reputation was on the line.

As I walked toward the school's main entrance, I spotted three anxious female faces peering out of the glass panes. The principal opened the door, led us to her office, introduced everybody, and got right to the point. "Terri is in the nurse's office. How do you want to handle this?" I said I would like to talk to Terri's teacher, Miss Monroe, to find out what Terri had told her. After that, I would like to speak with Terri in a private room. The principal escorted Miss Monroe and me to what looked like an oversized storage closet jammed with school supplies.

We sat on two metal folding chairs facing each other. Miss Monroe was young and pretty, her blonde hair pulled back in a ponytail, casually dressed in the latest fashion—the kind of teacher an impressionable third grader would idolize. We looked at each other and shook our heads. I broke the ice, "I taught third grade. That's some way to start a Monday morning!"

She gave a half-smile, "You can say that again! I was shaken up because of the blunt way Terri spilled out what happened. All she said was, 'I was raped on Friday night.' No emotion, no tears, no fear. She didn't seem a bit upset. I was so afraid of saying the wrong thing, that I excused myself and told Terri I would be right back before I hurried out to get help. That's about all I can tell you."

"You did the right thing by reaching out for help. Rape and Assault's role is to help guide you through this crisis. For openers, it would be helpful if you could tell me a little bit about Terri."

"She's a likeable child. She's outgoing, easy to talk to. She can be a little clingy at times though. She's an average student and tries hard to be liked. Terry craves attention. Her home life is shaky. Both of her parents work and she's left alone a lot." I thanked Miss Monroe for her input and asked her to send Terri in.

Terri bounced into the room as though she didn't have a care in the world, said a friendly hi, sat in the chair, and then gave me the once over. Her curly red hair encircled a fair-skinned face; her jade-green eyes were startling. She was tall for a third grader. She probably often got taken for being older.

As I observed Terri, my butterflies disappeared. I was in that familiar mode of one-on-one with a child who was hurting, one I knew I could help.

"Thanks for coming in to talk to me Terri. You don't know anything about me, so that wasn't easy to do. My name is Millie. It's my job to talk to children who say they've been touched in a way they don't like. I deal with…"

Terri snapped back, "I know why they want me to talk to you. It's because I told Miss Monroe I was raped. I told her because I saw on TV that you should tell someone if that happens to you."

"That's right. You're a smart girl. Do you think it's a good idea to have someone like me talk to children who were raped?" I always repeat a child's words; in this case I parroted her use of the word rape.

Terri shrugged her shoulders. "I guess so. But I wish I could of talked to Miss Monroe."

"That tells me you trust Miss Monroe a lot. She thought someone like me, who is trained to talk to children about these things, could help you more than she could. It's important that you know that she wants what is best for you. She cares about you. Miss Monroe is hoping that you will talk to me about what happened on the night you were raped."

"Will you tell her what I tell you?"

"That's up to you. If you want me to tell her, I will. If you don't want me to tell her, I won't."

"I want you to tell her. I want her to know. I won't tell you what happened unless you promise to tell Miss Monroe."

"I promise."

Terri maintained steady eye contact as we spoke. Her voice was strong. Her green eyes locked with mine. I hoped she knew my interest in her was sincere. My research, along with my contact with sexually abused children, had taught me that abused kids were very perceptive.

So far, I was pleased with the way our conversation was going. I sensed that Terri might be ready to spurt out what happened, without coaxing. For some reason, she seemed to want Miss Monroe to know what happened to her. But, unlike most child sexual abuse victims, she didn't appear traumatized. Sure enough, she blurted it out, with little hesitation and no visible emotion.

"It happened Friday night. I was bored so I dressed up as a rock star with lots of make-up. I wore bright red lipstick and jewelry. I hiked up my skirt. Stan—he's my step-dad, said I looked like a tramp. But what does he know? I loved singing some of Michael Jackson's songs in front of the mirror in my bedroom. Then my mom and Stan went to pick up some pizza and Jack and I were alone."

"Who's Jack?"

"He's Stan's cousin. He's nice. He kids around with me."

"How old is Jack?"

"I just went to his 21st birthday party."

"What happened while your mom and Stan were getting the pizzas?"

"Jack asked me to sit next to him on the couch. He had something for me. I went over. He put his arms around me and rubbed my back. I asked him what he had for me. He said 'Later.' Then he raped me."

"It would help if you could tell me exactly how Jack raped you."

"You know what I mean. He pulled down my pants, took out his sausage, and did it."

"Did what?"

"Rubbed it against my parts."

"What parts of yours did he rub against?"

"You know. My private parts—down there." Her finger pointed to her vaginal area.

"Thank you. I understand now. Exactly where did he rub his sausage on your private parts?"

"He pulled down my panties and rubbed it on the outside."

"Did he put his sausage inside you?"

"No. There wasn't time."

"About how long did he rub his sausage against your private parts?"

"Not long. When we saw their car headlights in the window Jack zipped up his pants and yelled at me to pull up my panties and pull down my skirt."

Terri stopped talking and we stared at each other in silence. She shrugged her shoulders. "That's it. That's what happened."

I sat there mesmerized by what she had told me. She kept glaring at me, seemingly without blinking. Relief suddenly swarmed through me when it sunk in that she had told me what happened. I quickly snapped back to reality and collected my thoughts. Terri's story sounded credible. The shocking part was her lack of embarrassment or emotion.

"That was a terrible thing Jack did. I'm very sorry he did something like that to you. What did you do next?"

"I sat up and pulled down my skirt fast. Then Jack and I sat and waited for them to come in. When they came in, I acted like nothing happened."

"Did you tell anyone about what happened with Jack?"

"No."

"How do you feel now about what Jack did?"

Terri shrugged her shoulders. "It's no big deal."

Was Terri as unaffected as her words implied?

"Some children might be upset if something like that happened to them. Did you feel upset?"

"No. Guys do that all the time."

"How do you know that?"

"My mom and Stan have videos of people doing it that I watch when I'm home alone."

"Had you ever seen a guy's sausage in real life before?"

"Lots of times. Stan walks around the house without any clothes on. He says people are dumb to make such a big deal out of it. He wiggles his sausage and says, 'I have something you don't have!' My mom laughs when he does that."

"How do you feel about Stan?"

"I HATE him. My mom and me were doing okay until he came along."

"How do you and your mom get along?"

"Pretty good—sometimes. But when me and Stan have a fight, she always takes his side. She loves him more than me."

"Do you see your birth dad?"

"No. He lives in Texas. He calls me on my birthday and Christmas and some other times. He'd see me a lot if he lived close but he has to live down there to make money to pay my mom child support. But I know he loves me very much."

"It sounds as though your dad is important to you."

"Yup. He's going to come for me someday."

Her vulnerability was touching and pulled at my heartstrings. However, it was time to re-focus on the sexual abuse.

"It seemed important to you that Miss Monroe knew you were raped."

For the first time, Terri was at a loss for words. She hung her head; she didn't move. I spoke softly. "Would you like to tell me why Miss Monroe means so much to you?"

Terri took a long time to answer. She slowly raised her head and looked me in the eye, whispering, "I have a make-believe world in my head. Do you know what that's like?"

"Yes I do. Does Miss Monroe live in your make-believe world?"

Terri shook her head yes. "I pretend she's my mom. She's kind. I'm always safe when she's there. No matter what happens, she takes me in her arms and tells me everything is going to be alright."

"Is that why you wanted her to know about your being raped?"

Terri nodded her head. "I knew she would feel bad and protect me. When I'm sad or scared, I go into my make-believe world and tell Miss Monroe all the bad things that happen to me and she still loves me. I'm happy in my make-believe world. My mom and Stan laugh at me; they say I'm a daydreamer."

"Sometimes a daydream world can be a safe place for an eight-year-old to go to for awhile. A make-believe place where wishes come true."

"Don't forget to tell Miss Monroe what I've told you."

"I won't. Can I share it with the others too?"

"If Miss Monroe says it's okay."

I tensed up. The time had come when, no matter how Terri felt about it, I had to tell her that I had to report what she told me to the police and a social worker. Would Terri feel betrayed? Angry? Scared?

"Terri. What Jack did was against the law because you are only a child. The police will want to talk with you about it. You don't have to be afraid of them. You did nothing wrong. They care very much about protecting children and will be very kind to you. They will think you are very brave to talk about it. They know that your bravery might stop Jack from doing the same thing to another child." I had learned that children care very much about other children and this often prompts them to disclose abuse. "Does that sound okay with you?"

Terri nodded her head. "I saw something like that on TV."

"Is it alright with you if I take you down to the nurse's office while I talk with Miss Monroe?"

"Yes."

"I'll talk with you again after I speak with Miss Monroe."

"Okay."

When I joined everyone in the principal's office, they were wide-eyed and hung onto my every word. I told them that I promised Terri that I would tell Miss Monroe what she told me. "Terri said it's alright if the rest of you know if that's what you want, Miss Monroe."

Miss Monroe nodded her head vigorously. "Absolutely."

As I told them what Terri had disclosed, they gasped several times and moaned in disbelief. Miss Monroe's eyes got misty. I thought about telling her about Terri's make-believe world but I wasn't sure whether Terri wanted me to so I played safe and didn't mention it. Above all, I didn't want to break a child's trust.

I explained to them that all cases of alleged child sexual abuse must be reported to either the police or the Division of Children and Youth Services (DCYS). "If you decide you want the police called, the detective will decide whether to call DCYS or come to the school himself to speak with Terri and then contact DCYS afterwards. When you decide which one you want contacted first, I will make the call and tell them what Terri told me."

The principal asked me to call the police. When I reached a detective, I related what Terri had told me. I later found out that this was his first child sexual abuse case. He said he would come to the school and take down Terri's statement. He wasn't sure about having an outsider sit in on a police investigation, on school property, without a parent having been notified. To play safe, he thought it best to do it privately. Understandable.

While we waited for the detective to arrive, Terri and I went back to our oversized closet. This time, she was a more subdued child. Less bravado. Those green eyes looked fearful. I asked how she was doing.

She yawned. "I'm tired. I fell asleep waiting for you to come back."

"I can understand why. Talking about things like this, not knowing what will happen next is scary, takes all your energy. I had one eight-year-old girl who was touched down there by a neighbor tell me that she slept until lunch time the next day after talking to me."

I told Terri that a detective would be coming in to talk to her and that I would have to leave; that was the law. She listened quietly and nodded her head. After the detective arrived and had spoken with the faculty members, he came to our room and we introduced ourselves. I was happy to see that he had a kind, compassionate expression on his face. I had a lump in my throat when I said good-bye. I gave Terri a hug and told her how brave she was, that she did something a lot of grownups were afraid to do. She gave me a little wave good-bye when I left.

The odds were that I would never see Terri again. Once the police reported the case to DCYS, confidentiality would take effect. Because I had had no contact with a parent, it was unlikely they would get in touch with me. I could only hope her parents understood why she had to tell and treated her with loving kindness. It was tough not being able to set up a child with counseling once she told me her story, a step I always take if at all possible.

The most heartening aspect of the case was that the message had seeped through to Terri to tell right after she was sexually abused.

That the veil of secrecy was slowly being lifted and others were becoming more aware of the problem and responding to it.

The detective on the case appreciated my contribution and called me back a few days later. He said Jack was a bundle of nerves and confessed soon after he was called in for questioning and read his Miranda Rights; a judge would sentence him. The police always prefer to question an alleged perpetrator before he contacts an attorney who advises him not to say anything, but that preferred scenario didn't happen often in the cases I handled.

Although I was pleased that Jack got caught and would be held accountable, I noted how his ignorance worked against him. Most offenders get a defense attorney before talking to the police and are then advised to plead not-guilty. That makes it a she said/he said case. Many times jurors say that they thought the defendant was guilty but the prosecution couldn't prove it beyond a reasonable doubt. It's difficult to find someone guilty only on the say-so of a child, with no physical evidence or corroborating witness.

Terri's case was the first of many I dealt with that came to Rape and Assault through the school system. I went on to interview children on all grade levels, each one presenting a unique set of challenges. Guidance counselors often made the initial phone call. They were leaned on heavily in almost every case and performed admirably. Without fail, the schools were cooperative and the authorities were notified after I spoke with a child.

15 Attorney General to the Rescue

As I continued to be privy to the initial disclosures of child sexual abuse, I became increasingly aware of the crucial need to videotape that fresh, raw testimony and reduce the number of times a child had to tell her traumatic story. Others involved in the criminal justice system could view the proceedings from behind a one-way mirror. Since DCYS and the police were often the first official responders, I suggested that they might be the ones to interview the child on videotape.

As mentioned earlier, I had been given an onsite tour of Colorado's innovative program, where they had a mandated set of protocols that everyone involved in child sexual abuse cases had to follow. It was designed to coordinate the efforts of all the professionals. The child's initial disclosure was videotaped. However, I was repeatedly told that wasn't the best way to handle these cases in New Hampshire.

In a state of maddening frustration, I mailed a proposal to our State Attorney General, Steven Merrill, citing the haphazard way child sexual abuse cases were processed in New Hampshire and the critical need for mandated protocols for those cases going through the Criminal Justice System. A few days later, his secretary called and set up a meeting.

When Deanna and I drove to Concord for the meeting, she told me about the first time she met Merrill. She was giving a radio interview on rape when he happened to leave the adjoining studio and overheard it. He stayed until the end, then introduced himself and told her how impressed he was with what she had said. I'm sure that chance meeting helped us to get this appointment.

I was both excited and nervous when Attorney General Merrill greeted us warmly. He was likeable and easy to talk to, traits that subsequently helped him become a popular two-term governor, one sensitive to women's issues. He was genuinely interested in what we had to say and asked pointed questions. Then he picked up the proposal I had mailed him and addressed me.

He said he liked the example I gave of a frantic principal who called Rape and Assault because a third-grade student told her teacher she was raped over the weekend and no one knew what to do. How they were waiting for me by the front door when I arrived to interview the child. He said he especially liked it when I said that when a third-grade student tells her teacher she was raped, there should be a set of mechanics in place so that everyone knew exactly what to do—a state-mandated protocol handed down from the Attorney General's office instead of each county playing by its own set of rules.

He stared at me before he continued. "This proposal is such good stuff. Why do you think you are having such a hard time getting anyone in the Criminal Justice System to listen to you?"

The dire weight of his words hit with a heavy thud and my voice sounded as weary as I felt. "I have agonized over that question. I don't know."

He leaned forward. "Did you ever consider that it might be because you live in a Republican, male-dominated, conservative state?"

I was stunned. "That thought never entered my mind."

Merrill said that the powers-that-be in the Criminal Justice System understood investigations and arrests. They were not tuned into new protocols dictated by female activists. I shook my head in disbelief. Merrill continued. He asked me how many women I came in contact with when I worked on cases that went through the Criminal Justice System.

"None. The police, county attorneys, defense attorneys, and judges are all men. I'm the lone female in meetings."

For the next two hours, Merrill, Deanna, and I brainstormed protocols that could be handed down from the attorney general's office, protocols that every law-enforcement official would be mandated to implement. Merrill ended our meeting on an upbeat note. He assured us that he was going to look into this matter and make changes in the way these cases would be prosecuted in the future. He ended by thanking us for bringing this issue to his attention and told us to keep up the good work.

Deanna and I were on an exhilarating high as we drove home. I was flooded with relief that the meeting had gone so well—so much had been riding on it. I sang the tune, *They'll Be Some Changes Made* as I bounced around in rhythm with the music. We treated ourselves to lunch and celebrated with a decadent brownie ice cream sundae.

In the coming days, I thought a lot about the attorney general's comments about living in a Republican, male-dominated, conservative state. I recalled how Deanna and I were the only women present when dealing with those in the criminal justice system, trying to bring about changes in the way these cases of child sexual abuse were handled. Because I now handled most of the cases and had more dealings with those in The System, I had to wake up to the reality that I had two strikes against me before I even opened my mouth.

I thought back to when I was the first female executive to crack the Marketing Department of a Manhattan, male-dominated publishing company. The words of Frank Sinatra's *New York, New York*, *"If you can make it there, you can make it anywhere."* made me smile. Perhaps Frank hadn't heard about New Hampshire being called the Nutmeg State—a tough nut to crack!

16 Videotaped at Last

I became disillusioned when months went by and we were still awaiting word from Attorney General Merrill on new protocols. I was also getting nowhere with the police, DCYS, or the county attorney's office about taping a child's initial testimony. I was in a spot I detested—stuck.

Utter frustration prompted me to make an impulsive offer to the Nashua Police Department. I suggested that when I received my next call about suspected child sexual abuse, I would call them before meeting with the child. The police could then set up videotape equipment in our office and a detective could be in the room when I interviewed the child. That way, the initial interview would become police evidence. They accepted the offer and I waited anxiously for my next call.

The following day, a call came in from a distraught mother, Kim, asking me to talk to her seven-year-old daughter, Casey, about possible sexual abuse by a young, casual friend of the family. I made an appointment to interview Casey the following morning. Kim gave me permission to have the interview videotaped. After we hung up, I gulped, picked up the phone, and dialed the number of the Nashua Police Department.

The next day, stomach cramps signaled the state of my nerves as I walked toward our office. The reality of what I had gotten myself into stopped me dead in my tracks as I watched two detectives carrying in the videotape equipment. What if the child won't open up to me? What if they accuse me of asking her leading questions? How much will I set back the cause if this doesn't work? My knees wobbled as I climbed the stairs to our office. The staff was edgy. We all knew how much was riding on this interview. Would the tape pass the test of being viewed by detectives, police chiefs, social workers, county attorneys, defense attorneys, and judges?

Detective X and his assistant arrived and set up the video equipment in my tiny office. They would position the camera to catch each of us on tape. When they were finished, the staff, the detectives, and I sat in tense silence and waited for Casey and Kim to arrive.

When Casey and Kim walked through the door, they had that familiar bewildered look of so many others who came before them. I rose and introduced everybody. I thanked them for coming in. I reiterated that Casey and her mom had given permission to have Casey's interview videotaped and I explained the set-up to everyone. Then Casey, Detective X and I went into the private room and shut the door. It was a stifling hot and humid day and the room had no air-conditioning. Detective X kept wiping off beads of perspiration with his handkerchief.

After we sat down, Casey startled me when she spoke first. "I don't want him in here when I talk to you."

"Casey, remember how we said that your testimony was going to be videotaped. Detective X is going to operate the camera. When you and I start talking, we'll forget he's here. He won't ask you any questions."

Casey folded her arms, sported a determined look, and stared into space. "I won't talk to you if he's in the room."

Detective X and I shrugged our shoulders and gave each other a look that said he was out of there. Then he said, "I'll set up the camera to focus on Casey's face. You can press the ON button when you're ready to start taping."

I asked Casey if that was okay with her. She finally looked at me. "Yes." When Detective X left, Casey and I read each other's faces in silence. I took a deep breath and pressed the ON button.

Casey's testimony followed a familiar pattern; I was comfortable with it. I used the skills I had learned from former victims to encourage her to open up. She was a delightful child and I took to her immediately. The presence of the camera in the room didn't change anything. In time, Casey reached the point where she revealed the sexual abuse, all felony charges.

When Casey's testimony ended, her body visibly relaxed. I then went into the supportive phase of the interview, the usual follow-up when a child discloses sexual abuse. I praised what she had the courage to do. She responded in a positive way and was greatly relieved that her story was out in the open. She was open to seeing a counselor. We had forged a strong connection.

I didn't realize how tense my body had been until it sunk in that the interview was over and I knew we had a "hot" video for the cause. I wished I'd had time to collapse with relief but we had a roomful of people anxiously waiting.

I pressed the OFF button and heaved a deep sigh. My knees were like jelly when I stood up. How hard this must be for a seven-year-old. But it's better than having her keep it bottled up inside for years. The counseling will help her deal with her trauma. She held my hand as we opened the door and faced wide-eyed, expectant stares.

"Casey and I are finished. She told me what happened."

The staff broke into grins from ear to ear. Detective X efficiently marked the videotape as police evidence and methodically packed up the equipment. Since the allegation happened outside Nashua's catchment area, he said that the Nashua Police Department would make a copy of the tape and deliver it to the police chief of the town where the alleged crime had been committed.

After the police left, Casey and I met with her mom and told her what Casey had reported. As usual, when the perpetrator is not a family member, parents are able to exercise the full brunt of their anger and demand that "we get the bastard." I explained that a detective and a DCYS worker would be in touch with them after they had a chance to view the tape. I told them how lucky they were that Casey's raw testimony was on videotape for the authorities to pursue instead of her having to tell her story over and over. They were happy about that.

When they left, Casey and I gave each other a bear-hug. When she asked if she could come back to talk with me again, I assured her she could. *Any time, Casey—any time.*

17 The Ocean

Driving home from my videotaped interview with Casey, I was emotionally drained, but thrilled that it had gone so well. Dick was on a business trip and I suddenly had an overpowering urge to drive to the ocean on such a hot, humid July day. I craved long walks on the beach to process the huge step that Rape and Assault had taken. At last, a child's initial interview had been videotaped and, at that very moment, was being viewed by those in the Criminal Justice System.

After I notified Dick and Rape and Assault that I was taking off for the seacoast, I threw a bathing suit, a toothbrush, and a few personal items in the car, slipped in an Elvis Presley tape, and headed east. I felt as free as the air.

After checking out the populated southern coast of Maine for several miles, the crowded beaches and exorbitant prices turned me off. Continuing to drive the scenic route north, I luckily discovered a secluded haven in Cape Porpoise, Maine, a picturesque fishing village, and fell in love with a small, cozy, $18 a night room in an old New England guest house overlooking the bay. I was enamored with its simple New England look—crisp white curtains, a spotless white twin bedspread, a small pine bureau, and a Boston rocker. Unbeknownst to me at the time, that room would become a haven whenever I hungered for an ocean respite from my work at Rape and Assault.

My emotions were still on high alert as I walked the village at sunset, cloaked in a foggy mist. I spotted a church steeple framed against the cloudy sky and, at that very instant, the sun broke through and lit up its steeple. I gasped at one of the most beautiful spiritual sights I had ever seen.

For dinner, I feasted on homemade clam chowder from a general store across the street that advertised it was George H. W. Bush's favorite when he was at his ocean retreat. After that, I snuggled in bed with a good book as I often gazed out the window at the bay filled with lobster boats, smelled the intoxicating sea air, and listened to the haunting sound of the foghorn. Peace enveloped me, allowing me to assimilate the day's events and fall into a deep sleep.

Refreshed, I got up at the crack of dawn and joined the lobstermen at their outdoor breakfast hangout on the dock. Those hard-working men were about to put in another long day on the water. With a strong Maine accent, they talked mostly about the weather and who caught what the day before. There were no wasted words. The normality of life was a welcome relief from the intensity of my work. After the boats headed out to sea, I walked the ocean's edge on isolated Goose Rocks Beach, swam in the cold Maine waters and lazily let the sun's warm rays soothe my tensed muscles.

When I headed back after two days, I felt rejuvenated. I realized how important my many travels on a shoestring budget were to offset these heavy-duty cases. I arrived home ready to go back to work.

I never saw the videotape of Casey's interview because I was walking the beach when the Chief of Police called Rape and Assault and asked to have me watch it with him. Deanna and Sandy went in my place and said that the Chief sat in stony silence as they watched it together. When it was over, he didn't move a muscle and sat in grim silence as he stared into space. He finally said, "She's good."

Deanna and Sandy were confused about who he was referring to. "Do you mean Casey?"

"No. The interviewer."

When I heard that, I said, "It's odd that he would focus on me rather than what the child said."

Deanna and Sandy replied, "Yea. We thought so too."

"Perhaps it was a shock for him to see that I could get a child that young to talk about sex in such minute, intimate detail."

Casey's case never went through the Criminal Justice System. Because the alleged perpetrator was a juvenile soon to turn eighteen, his case was handled in a confidential, juvenile court. In New Hampshire, juveniles' records are sealed when they turn eighteen years old, in order to give them a fresh start. I checked with the local juvenile authorities and they said that, although exceptions could be made, they were rare in cases of sexual abuse. Because many studies showed that juvenile offenders often become adult offenders, Rape and Assault continued to advocate for stiffer penalties for sexual offenders under the age of eighteen. Sure enough, many months later, I read in the paper that Casey's eighteen-year-old alleged offender had been arrested in a violent rape case.

As promised, her mom brought Casey in for several support visits. I explained to her why the case didn't come to trial, as well as the pros and cons of how juvenile cases are handled. I reinforced how her courage would help other abused children. Like most child victims, Casey showed an understanding beyond her years. I always spoke with a child as an equal. I had learned that kids can handle the truth a lot better than phony cover-ups.

Three months after our meeting with Attorney General Merrill, a large, manila envelope from his office came in the mail. I hugged it, closed my eyes, and prayed for good news. And good news it was! The attorney general had implemented many of Rape and Assaults' proposals and handed down mandated protocols to be followed when prosecuting child sexual abuse cases. Involved professionals would coordinate their efforts so that a child wouldn't have to tell her story over and over. In addition, the police and county attorneys would be attending training seminars on how to deal with those sensitive cases. As I read through the protocols, I said a silent prayer of thanks before I yelled out the good news to the staff. We all gave a loud "Yahoo!" Deanna and I got misty-eyed and gave each other a long, silent hug.

18 Everyone's Favorite Teacher

Fourteen-year old Jenny, and her mom, Brenda, were in their kitchen preparing supper for their family of six. They were talking about how, sometimes, we all do bad things. Jenny said, "I did something really bad in second grade." When Brenda asked what it was, she refused to talk about it, saying only that her second-grade teacher, Mr. X, made her and other kids do something really bad. Brenda asked if a friend, Cindy, had it happen to her too and Jenny nodded her head. After that, Jenny got livid when Brenda pressed her for more information. "I don't want to talk about it anymore." She stormed out of the kitchen, went to her bedroom, and slammed the door.

Brenda's instincts told her that something was very wrong. Jenny rarely blew up like that. She called Cindy's mom, Alice, told her what Jenny had said, and asked if she could shed any light on what might have happened. Alice didn't have a clue but she would ask Cindy about it. Her voice trembled when she called Brenda back. Cindy had admitted that something bad had happened but she absolutely refused to talk about it. The mothers were alarmed. What could Mr. X have done that was so bad they wouldn't even talk about it six years later?

Jenny was furious at her mom for blabbing to Cindy's mother. "I wish I never told you. Now the other girls are going to hate me." When pressed further, Jenny said it had to do with touching but the girls made a pact not to talk about it until they were sixteen years old.

A chill went down Brenda's spine. She had to do *something*. Who could she call at 6 p.m.? She decided to call the police for guidance. The detective on duty told her to bring her daughter in immediately for questioning. However, Brenda thought it would be too traumatic for Jenny to go in cold turkey like that. Then she remembered a program Rape and Assault had presented to parents at the school saying that parents had rights in how these cases were handled; they didn't have to rush right down to the police station just because they were told to.

I was mashing potatoes for supper when I got a crisis line call from a distraught mother named Brenda. I called Brenda back immediately, introduced myself, and asked how I could help her. "My daughter might have been touched in a bad way by a teacher. Oh, this can't be true. Mr. X was our favorite teacher. But I've never seen Jenny so upset. Can you help me—please—I don't know what to do."

I asked Brenda to start at the beginning and tell me what happened. In a shaking voice, she rattled off her story at a machine-gun pace. I could barely keep up with her as I took notes. Brenda continued. "I'm afraid that taking her to the police station would be too traumatic. Could someone from Rape and Assault speak to the girls before going to the police to find out what happened to them?" I explained that they were within their legal rights to do this and arranged for them to come to our office the following morning so I could talk to the girls. Brenda thanked me profusely and said they'd be there.

By this time, Jenny and Cindy knew they were going to be forced to talk about it. They contacted two other girls who were also in that second grade class and asked if they would join them when they went to Rape and Assault. One girl, Beth, agreed to come.

The following morning, when the mothers and girls arrived, they all looked bewildered. This was my biggest case as a volunteer and I hoped I didn't look as dazed as I felt as I mustered a professional demeanor. The three girls were cute, typical teenagers dressed in the latest denim fashion. The only thing that set them apart from most teenagers was the petrified looks on their mute faces.

As usual, I spoke with the mothers first. Because my office had barely enough room for my desk and three folding chairs, we huddled together. The mothers seemed like typical suburban homemakers, wrapped up in home and family, terrified about what they might hear. Being a mother myself, I empathized with their fears—that awful state when you anticipated hearing devastating news about your child. I addressed that fear while stressing how important their supportive role was if the girls were to reveal damaging secrets.

The mothers were in shock just thinking that something bad might have happened to their girls. Neither had slept the night before. They expressed warmth and admiration for the teacher, Mr. X, citing the extra attention he gave to needy students after school. He was a neighbor of Brenda's; he and his wife had been to their home for dinner, an evening they all enjoyed. They kept shaking their heads in disbelief. I could see the suspense was intolerable. "Why don't I talk to the girls now and try to find out what happened."

When we returned to the girls, each one seemed lost in her own thoughts. I gave them a choice of either talking to me alone or in a group. "It would be easier if we're together." (I found out later that I should have spoken to each one separately so as not to be faced with the charge that hearing someone else's testimony could have influenced what the others said.)

The four of us squeezed into my office. I started out by having each one tell me a little bit about herself, her home life, and her teenaged world. Even though they were pale and visibly shaken, they projected honest warmth; I responded to it. Then I told them about my background and how, as their advocate, I would be with them through whatever it was they had to face. I offered to answer any questions they might have. No one had one. They just stared at me, six eyes looking for a clue as to how to proceed.

After the initial warm-up, they relaxed a bit and we gradually approached the subject of their "bad secrets." They had shared little information about the details of what had happened to them in second grade. I stressed that nothing bad that an adult might have done to them was their fault. However, they were still leery to start talking. We discussed at length about how hard it was to keep bad secrets.

They cautiously opened up by testing the waters, revealing tiny tidbits of the nightmare that had haunted them for six years. As they slowly realized that the others had similar things done to them, they gradually cracked their heavily guarded defenses. Once the floodgates were opened, and they could finally talk about their dreaded secret, the individual stories came gushing out. It was bone-chilling to listen to them. They later gave me permission to disclose some of their testimony in order to give outsiders an inkling of what happened, keeping their identities secret.

"He placed his desk so no one could see what was going on behind it, even someone who walked in the room."

"He called me up to his desk to go over my paper with him. He pulled me close so no one could see what he did behind the desk. His hand went up my skirt and that's when he did it. I was so scared, I couldn't move. Even though I wanted to scream, I didn't make a sound."

"I started to cry and he put his arm around me to 'comfort me' and said for all the class to hear that I shouldn't be so upset over one grade on a paper. That I was sure to do better next time."

"The only one I could tell was my cat. I'd cry on my bed and my cat would sit in my lap and purr when I told her what happened."

"I begged my mom to let me wear slacks to school but back then the girls all wore dresses and she wouldn't let me wear my play clothes to school."

"He whispered in my ear that no one would believe me over a teacher if I tried to tell anyone."

"One time, I told the counselor that Mr. X might have done something bad to Dawn. After that, my mom was called and I heard her on the phone. 'Oh no!' over and over, each time getting louder, as she heard about what I had said. My mom agreed that Dawn had severe emotional problems, that she needed help, and how horrible it was for Mr. X to be falsely accused of something that awful.

"After my mom hung up, she gave me a hug and said I did the right thing to tell them what Dawn had said about Mr. X, but, of course, it wasn't true. That Dawn had emotional problems and they would see that she got the counseling she needed. She said how awful it was for him to be accused of such a horrible act. Then she said she gave permission for staff members to talk to me about it.

"The next morning, I was brought to the principal's office. The nurse and guidance counselor were there. They smiled at me. Then Mr. X put me on his lap. I hated sitting in his lap and almost started crying.

"They said I was right to tell about what Dawn had said. That Dawn had bad emotional problems which is why she said what she did. Then they asked me if Mr. X had ever touched me in a bad way. I figured they would say I had emotional problems too, if I told them. All I wanted to do was get off Mr. X's lap and go home. My heart was pounding so fast. I was too scared to tell them what he did when he called me up to his desk. So I lied and said no."

As the girls began to tell their stories, a look of sheer relief swarmed over their faces. Their eyes misted. They held hands. They were bubbly, as they savored their newfound freedom to talk about it. Beth was embarrassed because she couldn't stop laughing. I assured her that other children also react to trauma with hysterical laughter, that she didn't have to be embarrassed. They talked a lot about how hard it was to keep that secret for six years. There was an instant camaraderie among them for having shared such a tumultuous experience. When one spoke, the others nodded their heads as if to say they knew exactly how she felt.

"I was so afraid to have my parents find out that I'd done those dirty things."

"Mr. X was the most popular teacher in the school. No one would believe me over him."

"I didn't want the other kids in the class to know about those dirty things I did."

"My Dad said I was moody. He had no idea why."

"I still have nightmares about what happened when he kept me after school for extra credit."

However, amid their jubilation, silence crept in and hovered over the room when they faced the reality of their new situation. Their eyes took on the look of cornered animals.

"What happens now?"

"My parents are going to die when they find out. They think Mr. X is wonderful."

I validated their feelings. "It's going to be really hard to tell your parents about this. They'll be devastated. You need to give them time to absorb it. They are loving parents and, given time, should have the strength to get through it." At the thought of this, the girls became more subdued. Heavy eyes. Yawns.

It was time to move on, to meet with the mothers. "Would it be okay with you if we call in your moms now so we can tell them what happened? Once they know, we can talk about where we go from here." The girls looked at each other for confirmation and nodded their heads.

It was an emotion-packed drama when we broke the news to their moms, who were horrified beyond belief. There were tears and hugs as mothers and daughters embraced each other for support. It was chaos; everyone talked at once. It took the mothers a long time to absorb what they heard, to handle the shock. I gave them all the time they needed. I had to be sensitive to how much they could absorb before going onto the next step and, perhaps, spiraling them into overload.

When it was well past lunch time, I suggested we take a lunch break. As we sat around a table of a busy restaurant, the animated conversations and laughter of the lunchtime crowd filled the room. We must have been a sad, contrasting sight as we sat there, often in numbed silence, as we struggled to absorb, each in our own way, how all of our lives were now intertwined and forevermore changed. The mothers looked stupefied, glassy-eyed, and kept shaking their heads as if to say that they couldn't believe this was really happening. Because I knew their emotions were at the breaking point, I kept some thoughts to myself. I knew we were sitting on a keg of dynamite. Headline news. Ordinary people thrust into the limelight.

After a half-eaten lunch, we returned to Rape and Assault's office. Although exhausted, they hungered to know what would happen next. Like most citizens, none of them had any legal experience with the criminal justice system and had no idea how it worked. "Do we tell our story to the police and then they go out and arrest him?"

I spoke slowly so they could digest what I was saying. "What happens is that I will call the police and give the detective on duty the facts of the case. He will tell me when we should come in. Then we will all go down to the police station and a detective will question each girl. He will type up a police report as each girl testifies. This will take a long time as the police must be thorough and get all the exact facts, every bit of evidence. He may ask a question more than once for verification."

Then I reassured them that I would be there for support throughout the criminal process; they could call the answering service whenever they had a question and I would call them back. I explained that we didn't have to rush down to the police station and take immediate action, that they could talk things over among themselves and with their husbands/fathers first. When they felt ready to proceed, they could call me. At that time, I would call the Police Department and set up an appointment for all of us to meet there.

At this point there wasn't an ounce of energy left in any of them. It was time for them to go home, adjust to this nightmare that had shattered their peaceful, suburban lives, and speak with their husbands/fathers. I reiterated that there was no rush, to call me when they felt strong enough to go on.

Early the next morning, Brenda called and said they were ready to go to the police station. However, she wondered if I would come to her house first and talk with the fathers of the children. "The guys are fuming. They cried. My husband said it was incomprehensible; he couldn't deal with it. Another father said it was worse than serving in Vietnam. They want to beat Mr. X to a pulp."

At this point in the case, I gained confidence as I drove toward Brenda's home. Even though I was only a volunteer, I knew I was in a position to help guide them through this crisis. Rape and Assault's reputation gave me clout and Deanna's unfailing belief in my ability gave me the reinforcement I needed.

When I arrived at Brenda's home, the fathers were grim, with tightened jaws, in a state of disbelief. As the protectors of their families, a father's instinct is to "kill the bastard." While I empathized, I said their girls needed strong dads by their sides, not ones in jail for murder. In all my years with Rape and Assault, I never had one father who took the law into his own hands, which amazes me to this day, given the raw, repressed rage that burns inside of them.

When their many questions were answered, they were ready to proceed. When I called the police, I was connected to a detective. When he heard the allegations, his voice had a sense of urgency and he said to come in *right now*.

From the moment we entered the police department, the case was given top priority. The detective greeted us warmly, and introduced himself to each one personally. As he paraded us through the police station, all eyes were on us, in hushed silence.

After the detective made sure we were comfortable, offered us coffee or soda, and showed us where the restrooms and snack machines were, he said he would speak to each girl separately. So began the long, arduous process of taking down the girls' statements.

The detective was thorough, professional, kind, and patient, displaying little emotion as the girls revealed the sordid details. Most detectives had children of their own and many told me their emotions boiled inside of them whenever they were on the hunt for predators who sexually abused kids. I could sense that rage, so well hidden behind the detective's stony face. The veins alongside his forehead were pulsating.

As I witnessed the girls' courage, I vowed to fight for them with every ounce of energy I had. Although terror-stricken, they knew they were doing the right thing. That proved more important than the fear and embarrassment of others, especially peers, finding out about the dirty things that had been done to them when they were seven years old. They would be strong witnesses. They had to be in order to survive the ordeal that faced them.

Completing the testimonies and holding family conferences took up most of the day. When the detective finally had all the information he needed, his voice cracked ever so slightly when he expressed his thanks and gratitude on behalf of the police department for their testimonies. By day's end, everyone was bleary-eyed, running on an empty tank.

Because of the alleged severity of the case and the fact that time was of the essence, the County Attorney's Office was notified immediately. There was a second grade teacher out there who might be molesting other girls. As was so often true, the girls wanted to protect other children from the abuse they had endured, a powerful motivating factor in their decision to press charges. At thirteen years old, they finally had the strength to confront Mr. X and, hopefully, put him behind bars.

In New Hampshire, the County Attorney is a constitutionally elected official and the chief law enforcement officer in the county. His office is staffed with Assistant County Attorneys. After the County Attorney read the preliminary police report, he called each family and asked them to come in for questioning. He assigned the case to an Assistant County Attorney, Prosecutor X, who told me many years later that it was the most important case of his career.

Once again, the girls and their parents made a strong first impression. It was clear that these were law-abiding, hard-working citizens with no ax to grind. That fate had struck them a devastating blow and they were struggling to cope with it as well as reporting it to the authorities. They projected both an internalized pain and a steadfast conviction that they were going to do whatever it took to make Mr. X pay for what he did.

When the girls' stunning testimonies were completed, Prosecutor X could see that he had strong, committed witnesses. The parents and girls were adamant that this crime be made public. They wanted people to know that this horrendous crime had happened to ordinary families whose parents were very involved in their children's lives, parents who sent their children off to school with the words, "Pay attention to the teacher and do what the teacher says." They also wanted to provide living proof that young children can be terrorized into secrecy by a trusted authority figure.

The County Attorney's Office had never handled a child sexual abuse case of this magnitude. They appreciated my contributions and treated me as an equal professional. We shared input on an ongoing basis. Although hardened to crime, they could hardly fathom that a respected second grade teacher was capable of such heinous acts.

Throughout the 1980's, Rape and Assault, with Deanna as the main spokesperson, fought ferociously for changes that would help ease the trauma of a child going through an adult-oriented criminal justice system. She testified for new legislation that was enacted on an ongoing basis. However, many of the laws that are on the books today were not in effect when this case was prosecuted. Therefore, it proceeded under some archaic laws.

For example, at one point early in the process, it looked as though an existing statute was going to bring the case to a screeching halt. The statute stated that an alleged victim of child sexual abuse had less than six years from the date of the alleged crime to press charges. Because the abuse happened just over six years ago, the Statue of Limitations had run out. We were all sick to our stomachs.

However, a stroke of luck saved the day. The statute also said that if an alleged perpetrator had moved from the state while the Statute of Limitations was in effect, he would be considered a fugitive from justice and the Statute of Limitations didn't apply. Because Mr. X had taken a teaching job in another state, he could still be charged with the crime. Later on at a congressional hearing, Deanna cited this case as living proof that child sexual assault victims needed a longer period of time to come forward. As a result, new legislation was passed (in increments) to extend the Statute of Limitations. Today a child sexual abuse victim has until the age of thirty-two to report a crime. Currently, thirteen states have no Statute of Limitations.

Prosecutor X made arrangements for a detective to serve Mr. X a warrant for his arrest. The clock ticked ever so slowly as we anxiously awaited news. Would he fight the arrest? Deny the allegations? Think he was off the hook after the Statute of Limitations had run out? The detective told us later that he had served Mr. X the warrant as he left the school building at the end of his teaching day. He offered no resistance, and meekly went into custody.

The mothers and girls decided to attend the arraignment so the girls could get used to seeing Defendant X now that they were teenagers. That way it wouldn't be such a shock when they faced him at trial. We met in the waiting room at Superior Court. One girl had a bad stomach ache, one didn't sleep the night before, and one threw up waiting for the arraignment to begin. They clung to their moms, behavior more similar to that of seven year olds, the ages they were at the time of their abuse.

We entered the courtroom in hushed silence, sat down front, and waited for Defendant X to appear. When the side door opened and he slowly entered, I stared at him, looking for some clue that might give a hint of his evil character. However, he looked like your average male, with a well-trimmed haircut, and dressed neatly in a conservative suit and tie. His stone-faced expression showed no emotion as he walked in like a zombie and took his place at the table next to his attorney, facing the judge's chair. *What caused you to do such despicable acts? Do you feel remorse? Was the sick thrill worth the price you are going to pay? Do you come from an abusive background like most offenders?*

Not a sound came from the mouths of the girls or parents. We were all frozen in time as we waited for the judge to enter the courtroom. When the door to his chamber opened and a somber-looking judge appeared, we all rose as he took his seat on the bench. The court was now in session.

One of "due process" rights in an arrest is the right to be told exactly what you are accused of, at the arraignment. The judge read the charges against him. Then he asked the defendant if he understood the charges.

He mumbled a soft, "Yes."

When Defendant X then pled Not Guilty to the charges, those two words meant that the case would go to trial. The prosecutor would have to prove beyond a reasonable doubt that Defendant X did what the girls said he did.

The arraignment happened so fast, we could hardly process that Defendant X was ushered out and it was over. We stared at each other in silence.

However, when we returned to the lobby, the girls found their voices. They weren't clinging to their mothers anymore. "It was scary to see him again." "I felt more like seven years old than thirteen." However, all were more determined than ever that he was going to pay for robbing them of their childhoods. "When he said 'Not Guilty,' I wanted to shout out, 'LIAR!' " "I'm scared to death to go to trial but I couldn't live knowing he had gotten away with it because I was too scared to face him. I couldn't do it when I was seven years old but he's going to find out that I can do it when I'm thirteen." I was encouraged to hear their angry outbursts; anger is often a healthy motivating force that enables victims to get through the trauma of a trial.

The next step in the legal process was the Probable Cause Hearing. This is a preliminary hearing that typically takes place after the arraignment and before a serious crime goes to trial. The judge is presented with the basics of the prosecutor's case and the defendant is afforded full right to be represented by legal counsel. If the prosecution cannot make a case of Probable Cause, the court must dismiss the case against the accused. In this case, there was overwhelming evidence. Three girls accused him of sexual abuse so it was more than a he-said, she-said situation. As expected, the judge found Probable Cause.

The legal process now entered the agonizing, "dragging on" stage. It is a long, laborious process for each side to prepare a case for trial. Also, defense attorneys use every trick in their legal bag to postpone trial dates, hoping that child victims will cave in under the pressure of waiting and be more apt to accept a watered-down plea bargain.

One time, I had the opportunity to question a defense attorney about the ethics of taking advantage of a child. I was alone in an employee court lounge when a successful defense attorney walked in. I introduced myself, and impulsively asked him, "Do you ever feel guilty about taking such unfair advantage of children on such an unleveled playing field?"

He replied with an emphatic "NO. It's my job to make the prosecuting attorney work as hard as I can to get a successful conviction. If a jury finds my client not guilty, it's because the prosecuting attorney didn't prove his case beyond a reasonable doubt. I force them to become better prosecutors and the children win out in the long run. If they think there is a loophole where I can take unfair advantage of a frightened child, then it's their job to work on getting the loophole fixed."

I contemplated his words. "I never looked at it that way. We at Rape and Assault fight for changes in how these cases are prosecuted and have gotten many statutes overturned. However, sometimes we're unsuccessful even though the need is great."

"Can you give me an example?"

"We're not getting anywhere in getting an Incest Diversion Program. County Attorneys don't want to look soft on crime. It would be tougher for you to get a Not-Guilty verdict for incest fathers if the County Attorney's Office implemented an Incest Diversion Program."

"That's a perfect example of what I was talking about."

He ended our conversation with a little humor. "When my kids read about a trial in the newspaper, they ask, 'How come you never work for the good guys?'" Today, this same defense attorney is a judge and from what I hear and read in the paper, he hands down tough sentences. I'm sure he points that out to his kids!

As Defendant X's case dragged on, the mothers said the wait took its toll on the girls. Grades dropped. Like most thirteen-year-olds, they wanted more than anything else to fit in with their peers. Would their classmates figure out that they were the victims who did those dirty things when the case came to trial? Be embarrassed to hang around with them?

One of them had recently won a statewide beauty/talent contest but she didn't feel beautiful anymore now that the other kids might see her as damaged property. However, never once did any one of them mention backing out. They were determined to have their day in court and expose Mr. X for everyone to see. They wanted him barred from teaching forever. The fortitude of the girls and parents earned my respect, something I repeatedly told them.

The girls were especially afraid to give their depositions because I had warned them that defense attorneys had free reign to ask whatever they wanted, with no supervision, and often tried to intimidate young victims. We practiced how they should take their time answering questions, always telling the truth. Saying "I don't know" rather than guessing at an answer. They did very well in their depositions; their words reeked of truth. One example of how Deanna and Rape and Assault worked hard to bring about legislative changes occurred after Deanna's testimony before a Senate Select Hearing. Following her testimony, a law was designed to protect children under age 16 from repetitive subjection to interrogation without judicial supervision by barring discovery depositions of victims and witnesses who were under 16 years of age at the time of an offense.

Many agonizing months after the girls first walked into the Rape and Assault office, the day of the trial finally arrived. On the day they were to testify, the girls waited in the County Attorney's Office until it was their turn to take the stand. The tension level for everyone involved was insufferable but the strength of the girls and their families was steadfast.

Because the case involved minors, the courtroom was closed to outsiders when the girls testified. However, they asked that I be the only one allowed in the courtroom during their testimony. They felt that having their parents present would be too emotional and might cause them to break down on the stand. "Millie will give us support." I was relieved that I was allowed to be present so I could watch firsthand what transpired.

I opened the heavy door to the courtroom, slowly walked down the aisle, and took a seat in the front row. The attorneys were in their respective places. I stole a look at Defendant X but it was hard to read his face as it was void of all emotion.

When Prosecutor X called the first girl to testify, a hushed silence permeated the room. I turned my head to the doorway. I will never forget the sight of the big door opening up and seeing Jenny's delicate frame outlined in the door frame. She walked down the aisle with her head held high as we had practiced and our eyes locked as she passed by. She had the faintest wisp of a resigned smile. I got a lump in my throat and blinked away tears. I was so proud of her.

At long last, the questioning began.

Jenny was as strong as she had been during the practice sessions. Her voice broke when she described the sexual abuse but she got through it. The courtroom was so quiet, I could hear myself breathe. The jury sat there stone-faced. Defendant X's face didn't move a muscle. Jenny's words rang true. She was also strong on cross-examination. When she was excused from the stand, I gave a prayer of thanks as she walked past me. Our eyes met and expressed our grave relief.

Beth was the next witness. She had been kept after school for "extra help." My stomach was in knots because I knew the shocking story she had to tell about what happened, the degrading acts she was terrorized into doing. She was emotional even in the practice sessions. She was the one most likely to break down on the stand.

Prosecutor X asked her easy questions to get her used to hearing her voice in the courtroom. As he gradually worked up to the heavy duty stuff, her voice cracked but she was getting through it. Although I had heard her story many times, it still had the power to blow my mind. Everyone in the courtroom seemed transfixed as though they could hardly believe what she was saying.

Partway through her testimony, Defendant X whispered something in his attorney's ear who then requested a recess, which the judge granted. When the trial resumed, Defendant X's attorney addressed the court to say that his client wanted to enter a guilty plea.

Just like that, it was over. We later learned that, even though it was not visibly apparent, Defendant X didn't want to hear any more. Plus, I knew that there was worse to come and perhaps he saw that Beth was strong enough to get through it.

Pandemonium broke out after the guilty plea—bodies poured into the courtroom. Everyone speaking at once. News reporters and TV cameras appeared from all directions, each one vying for the limelight. Somehow, through it all, the girls, parents, and I found each other and we hugged, laughed, and cried, with long sighs of relief that the nightmare was finally over. The girls' courage had allowed justice to triumph and sent a strong message that those secret walls surrounding child sexual abuse were being smashed.

On the day of sentencing, we all sat down front with a strong sense of having done the right thing. The courtroom was packed with reporters. While waiting for the judge to appear, people came in and whispered in the reporters' ears. Many journalists hurried out. I couldn't imagine what was happening. We were soon to find out that the space ship Challenger, carrying Christie McCullough, a New Hampshire school teacher, had blown up during take-off.

The next day, the tragic story of the Challenger took up the entire front page of the Nashua Telegraph except for one small box on the bottom right of the page: *New Hampshire Teacher Sentenced to Twenty-two years.*

Such irony. The bad teacher lived and the good teacher died.

19   Inside a Jail

The two steadfast mothers, Brenda and Alice, wanted to see the jail where Mr. X would serve his time so they could visualize how he would suffer behind bars and they asked me to go along. When we arrived, the warden greeted us warmly and appointed a guard to take us on a personal tour.

To me, being locked up would be a supreme form of torture. The visions of that day remain imprinted in my mind. Twenty-four hours a day, prisoners are stripped of all privacy. There are no doors, not even in the bathrooms. Security cameras monitor their every move. There are two prisoners to a cramped cell, void of everything but the barest necessities. Some prisoners were lying motionless on their cots staring at the ceiling. Others had deadened looks on their faces as they stared at us through the bars as we walked by. As we strolled through the eerily-quiet jail blocks, I wished that juvenile delinquents were mandated to get a tour of a jail, in case they were considering a life of crime.

During the tour, Alice commented that the fragrant odor of home baked bread throughout the jail bothered her; she said it was more than they deserved. It turned out that the prisoners baked the bread themselves and this saved the state money. However, Alice wasn't ready to grant them that pleasure.

The subject came up about how other prisoners detested child molesters above all and often raped them in order to give them a taste of their own medicine. I wondered how that was possible and questioned the guard, "You said that a camera is on them 24 hours a day. How do they get away with it?" Brenda, Alice and the guard gave me a quizzical look that questioned why I needed to ask that. I quickly understood why many jails have separate quarters for child molesters.

Driving home, Brenda and Alice said that seeing the jail had given them some closure. They could now envision Mr. X spending twenty-two years behind bars for his heinous crimes against their daughters.

20 Good Day! Show

The stalwart mothers, Brenda and Alice, were contacted to appear live on the morning network TV show *Good Day!* to discuss the case, and they asked me to join them. Even though I was terrified at the prospect, it was something I had to do—this was my chance to educate the public. Panic set in because, as the professional spokesperson, I *had* to know the answer to every question they asked.

I watched the show in advance to case their format. The first guest was a handsome soap opera actor with a toothy smile who sat on their pink couch with his legs crossed and his arm casually draped over the back. He didn't look a bit nervous. The second guest was a detective who was obviously as petrified as I was going to be. He sat with his body stiffly erect, eyes frozen straight ahead, and his arm clutched tightly to the arm of the couch. I vowed that no matter how scared I was, my body was going to look relaxed.

In preparation, I had also made up pink index cards covering what I thought would be the most important questions. Every spare minute, I practiced going over those questions and answers. I saw those pink index cards in my sleep.

When Brenda, Alice, and I drove to the TV station, we gabbed in the car as usual. But after parking, we walked to the entrance in solemn silence. Live television! "Please God," I prayed, "Let me get the words out of my mouth and not stutter. Please don't let my mind go blank when I'm asked a question. Please don't let me have a coughing fit."

When we met the hosts of the TV show for a twenty-minute warm-up, one female crew member said that she had been molested by her father and was thrilled they were airing this program. Then they whisked us into the studio, fitted us with microphones, and seated us on that couch. Matching pink index cards flitted nervously through my head. The director quieted us by counting down from ten.

"Good morning."

Eileen, the moderator, opened with background information about the case. Then she startled Brenda by asking her to tell the audience how it all happened. Brenda quickly recovered and started telling the story from the beginning.

Alice spoke next and did a great job in her usual calm, controlled manner. They were coming through as typical mothers-next-door, who wanted to warn parents that something this horrible could happen to them.

At last Eileen asked me a question. Oh happy day. It was one that I'd put on a pink card. My vocal chords worked. I didn't stutter. I didn't have a coughing fit. I was talking on live TV! As it turned out, I had made out a card for every question she ended up asking me.

Twenty minutes later, with one commercial break, our *Good Day!* interview was over. We had gotten our message across. Driving home, we were giddy with relief that we hadn't blown it. When I watched the videotape later, I was surprised by how calm I looked though my heart had been pounding. We came across as three ordinary citizens with compelling stories to tell.

At 6 a. m. the following morning, I was awakened by a phone call from an out-of-town friend who had been sexually abused as a young child. She hadn't known that the show was being aired. However, that night she fell asleep with the TV on. She told me she woke up from a sound sleep at 2 a. m. hearing my voice in the background. There I was on her TV screen! The station had rebroadcast the show. She watched it mesmerized, pleased at the work I was doing. Some coincidence. Or, as I had so often asked myself, "What's going on with all these 'coincidences'? Is there something a little bit spooky going on here?"

Ever after, those pink cards had an honored place in my reference file. My next request was to serve on a panel in Boston with Gloria Steinem, and with my pink companions in tow, I confidently headed south to be part of the program. I drove home on a high from the Gloria Steinem experience. There was no role I loved more than that of a teacher.

However, sadly, I knew I still did not possess the skills or self-confidence to present a public speaking presentation on my own.

21 From Volunteer to Staff Member

After five years as a volunteer, I had struck a good balance between my work at Rape and Assault and my personal life.

Whenever I had free time, I gave my volunteer work with the agency top priority and arrangements were made to have all child sexual abuse cases forwarded to me at home. If I was unavailable, Deanna handled the calls. I also gave hands on training to three carefully selected volunteers who were giving us much needed relief.

This arrangement afforded me the flexibility I needed. Dick was retired and we wanted the independence to travel together—a month on the Keys, three weeks in Maine, along with other spontaneous trips. In addition, I was bitten by the travel bug more than Dick and often took exciting solo adventures on a shoestring budget.

It was at this point that Deanna approached me with an offer. She felt my work was crucial to the running of the agency and wondered if I would consider signing on as a staff member—to become Rape and Assault's first Child Sexual Abuse Coordinator. It would be a part-time position—twenty hours a week—minimum pay—no benefits.

I weighed the offer carefully. I wanted to be certain that accepting it would be in the best interests of both the agency and myself. The offer appealed to me because, one, I would gain more clout in the community as a staff member and, two, it would relieve Deanna's workload as she juggled the needs of a fast-growing agency.

However, I was certain of one thing: At this stage of my life, I was not going to tie myself down fifty-two weeks a year for a part-time job.

I explained to Deanna that I would be willing to give the agency the equivalent of twenty hours a week, or one-thousand-forty hours a year, as long as I could space them out in a way that allowed me to travel. I told her that without that guarantee, I would prefer staying on as a volunteer. Deanna agreed to my terms and drew up a contract, which I signed.

I started my new job on April 1. Even though I had entered the office countless times as a volunteer, it felt strange walking there as a staff member. When I reached the office, my co-workers shouted out in unison, "APRIL FOOL! We were only kidding!" That broke the ice.

After a good laugh, I walked to my desk and settled in. I shared a tiny room with Julie. Space was so tight we could hardly maneuver into our chairs. Because so much of our work was done on the phone, we had to get used to hearing two simultaneous conversations. As my first day progressed, it seemed both surreal and natural. Later on when I joined the others for a Court Sentencing Hearing, I kept thinking I was getting paid for doing something I was used to doing for free.

In time, I grew to enjoy my new role and to be part of the innumerable discussions that spontaneously ensued. I gained a renewed appreciation for how hard everyone worked and the high caliber of their efforts. My caseload rose as more victims poured in. As my reputation grew in the community, I increasingly became a spokesperson for the agency, a role I relished as education was my greatest passion.

I kept track of my hours and put in one-thousand-forty hours per year as we had agreed. However, as time wore on, unbeknownst to me, some staff members felt I was being given favorable treatment in that I could pick and choose my work hours. They needed someone in the office they could depend upon each week to handle the child sexual abuse calls.

One Monday morning when I returned to work relaxed after a month on the Keys, sporting a glowing tan, a new contract greeted me on my desk. In a cover letter, Deanna said that while I was gone a staff meeting had been called to discuss my work schedule. As a result of the meeting, it was decided that, to meet the needs of the agency, my services were needed twenty hours each week.

Although I could understand their position, my decision was instantaneous. After reading the contract, I immediately went to the front office where the entire staff awaited my reply. I reiterated that I would not tie myself down fifty-two weeks a year for a part-time job. That, in the best interests of the agency, they should consider hiring someone who could meet those requirements and I would go back to being a volunteer.

Silence filled the air after I spoke. Deanna finally said she would readdress the issue and get back to me. I said that was fine and I went back to my desk to resume my work. After a deep breath, I was surprised at how calm I was as I sorted through the accumulated mail. Although I felt a stinging disappointment at the possibility of losing my status as a staff member and thus not being able to fulfill the many goals I had hoped to achieve to better the cause of child sexual assault, I knew it was an irrevocable decision.

After reassessing the situation, Deanna said the agency would stick to the original agreement. Even though the subject was never brought up again, I am sure there was some continued resentment at my free-wheeling schedule. However, I was comfortable with the arrangement as I felt I had been allowed to be honest and forthcoming about my position.

I went on to serve seven years as a staff member.

22 Training the Professionals

Although many staff members at Rape and Assault did train and educate professionals about the child sexual abuse issue, there was a dire need for those involved in the prosecution of these cases to be trained by leading experts in the field. To help achieve this goal, I researched successful national programs.

I was excited when I discovered *The National Children's Advocacy Center (NCAC)* in Huntsville, Alabama. Formed in 1985, it was the first organized effort to create a better system to help abused children. They recognized that the social service and criminal justice systems were not working together in an effective manner, a gap that added to a child's emotional distress and created a segmented, repetitious, and often frightening experience for the child. The NCAC's advocacy model pulled together law enforcement, criminal justice, child protective services, and medical and mental health workers onto one coordinated team.

Reinforced with materials from the *NCAC* program, as well as others, Deanna and I met with the Hillsborough County Attorney and his subordinates to discuss the need for implementing training programs. The timing was right, because after Deanna and I had met with Attorney General Merrill, he had officially mandated child sexual abuse training for all those in the criminal justice system.

Rape and Assault's efforts helped create the *Hillsborough County Attorney Task Force on Child Sexual Abuse*. This Task Force led to the County Attorney's Office sponsoring a Three-Day Workshop on Child Sexual Abuse that featured our preferred presenters. Deanna and I were psyched.

However, I arrived home from Colorado the day before the workshop began with a 103 degree temperature. Undaunted, I jammed some medicines in my pocketbook and took off for the County Attorney's Office.

When I walked into the conference room, an emotional high and a heavy dose of aspirin overrode the physical effects of my raging fever. As I walked toward the seat Deanna had saved for me down front, I absorbed the awesome energy of the audience encompassing all the disciplines—law enforcement, criminal justice, child protective services, and medical and mental health workers. When the meeting got underway, the outstanding speakers, the wealth of information, and the stimulating question and answer periods were exhilarating.

Even the onset of a category 3 hurricane on the last day of the conference that had the County Attorney's ear glued to a weather report for immediate evacuation, failed to dampen the success of the workshop. Knowing what a turning point this was in how New Hampshire would handle these cases in the future filled me with such a powerful inner glow that, sometimes, I just closed my eyes, tuned everything out, and gave thanks that this was really and truly happening. Even my fever broke in celebration.

That workshop was the forerunner of many future training sessions. They were often sponsored by individual disciplines, which gave in-depth perspectives of their unique roles in the overall process. Deanna and I sponsored one for Rape and Assault. A particularly interesting one for me was given by the first female Superior Court Justice, Linda Delanis, who shared the dilemmas a judge encountered when trying these cases. These personalized workshops gave everyone a bird's-eye view of the problems we faced.

At this point, I thought I was pretty shockproof. However, one workshop proved me wrong. The staff of Rape and Assault had been invited to attend a three-day seminar on child abuse sponsored by the Attorney General's office, one geared toward hardened law-enforcement personnel. Nothing prepared me for what I saw on confiscated videotapes. They were tapes that the perpetrators had videotaped themselves because they wanted to experience the thrill of watching them again. I forced myself to view them as I wanted to know just how bad it got for some children. The sick pleasure on the faces of the perpetrators during their sadistic sexual abuse acts was nauseating. Sometimes, the physical abuse was even worse. The vision of a perpetrator putting a child's hand on a hot stove burner still haunts me.

Although Rape and Assault operated on a barebones budget, Sandy squeezed out money for staff to attend ongoing conferences. Since I was becoming their authority on child sexual abuse, I often attended the ones on this topic, making copies of printouts and my summarized notes for the staff. The entire staff attended an outstanding, four day seminar on child sexual abuse offered by the Harvard Medical School. These high quality programs were money well spent because they helped us become more effective advocates and better informed educators.

These conferences reinforced Rape and Assault's belief that child sexual abuse was a community problem best solved with a community approach. This awareness led to the formation of *NETWORK*, an organization comprised of professionals involved in the handling of child sexual abuse cases. *NETWORK* members met once a month and this organization became a leading voice in developing coordinated solutions. When I won their annual award for my work with sexually abused children, it was an honor I humbly cherish to this day.

After developing its innovative team approach on the local level, my original role model, the *National Children's Advocacy Center (NCAC)* in Huntsville, Alabama went on to earn a national reputation, and they used it to train others to deal effectively with this critical problem. Today, more than 54,000 child abuse professionals have been trained by the *NCAC* and there are now more than 600 child advocacy centers in the United States, including several in the state of New Hampshire.

23 Speak Up! Say No! Tell Someone!

Rape and Assault was encouraged that professionals now had access to training programs on how to best handle cases of child sexual abuse. Nevertheless, we continued to keep abreast of upcoming workshops and shared this information with relevant organizations. It was especially heartening to observe the coordinated efforts among the various disciplines that had one goal in mind: how to ease the trauma for a child who alleges sexual abuse.

Now that we had that going for us, we could concentrate on another major offensive: Preventive Education. We never lost sight of the fact that education is the key to combating this crime. Such a breakthrough would teach children how to SPEAK UP! SAY NO! TELL SOMEONE! if they were approached or touched in a way that made them uncomfortable.

Sandy Matheson, our Program Director, realized that the best way to accomplish this would be to create and implement quality educational programs as part of the school teaching curriculum, ones specifically designed for each grade level. When she finally felt ready to take action, she knew it was imperative to sell this innovative proposal to every rung of the educational ladder including parents, school boards, teachers, principals, supervisors, and superintendents.

As always, Sandy was well prepared with a top-notch curriculum in place for each grade. To help sell the package, she offered to present the classes herself rather than place an added burden on overworked teachers, a major reason why the teachers were so willing to have it adopted. Getting the program into the schools was a slow, step-by-step process, but she progressively won over converts.

Even though this was a serious, delicate undertaking, Sandy always had funny stories to relate which added some levity to the seriousness of the situation. In one kindergarten class, she had shown the movie, *Penelope Mouse*, and in response to her question about what a diary is, a little boy answered, "A diary is when you have to go poop so bad and you can't hold it and it all runs down your leg."

Nashua eventually mandated that these preventive programs be given in grades kindergarten through high school, and several surrounding communities followed suit. We at Rape and Assault considered this one of our highest achievements.

Sandy and her successors, Debbie and Cecile, broadened the outreach and offered numerous educational programs throughout the community—PTO's, Women's Clubs, Rotaries, Girls Clubs, Boys Clubs, health professionals, senior citizens, church groups, college courses, clergy, law enforcement—in short, anyone who wanted to learn about ways to help prevent child sexual abuse. Those dedicated staff members were tireless pioneers whose innovative breakthroughs would help improve the lives of women and children for generations to come.

I continued to feel grateful that I was working for such a highly esteemed agency that shared my goals.

24   Public Speaking Jitters

Because of my growing expertise in the field of child sexual abuse, I encountered increasing pressure from the staff at Rape and Assault to present programs to share my knowledge.

However, because I had stuttered earlier in my life, the dread of it recurring in front of a live audience paralyzed me. It made little difference that I had slowly resolved my stuttering problem as I grew into adulthood. I didn't want to risk it as a public speaker. How I wished I could because I knew my experience in the trenches would be a valuable educational tool.

I had faced my fear when I appeared on live TV with the mothers of the *Everybody's Favorite Teacher* case because I felt compelled to grab that chance to educate thousands of viewers. However, that one incident did not overcome my terror of public speaking.

Finally, I decided I needed to take another step so I took a course in Public Speaking at the New Hampshire Vocational Technical College. At age fifty-eight, I was easily the oldest student. We classmates were sensitive to each other's anxieties about speaking before an audience and helped one another work through them. One piece of wisdom we received stuck with me: "If you're too nervous to speak in public, perhaps you are self-conscious. It could be that worrying about your image is more important than your message."

After that class, I worked on overcoming my fear. I started out by sitting in on Sandy's and Debbie's presentations. As I sat silently on the stage, they introduced me as Rape and Assault's Child Sexual Abuse Coordinator who managed the bulk of the agency's cases. Unexpectedly, because of my hands-on experience with the victims, many questions from the audience were directed to me and I could no longer sit in silence. Once I realized I could answer without stuttering, self-confidence slowly overrode my terrors and I began to share my knowledge.

After those victories, I gradually took on guest speaker engagements. But not before I had developed a well-scripted, comprehensive, opening presentation that I could recite by heart. I especially enjoyed the enlightenment of the question and answer period. Knowing that education was a key component to winning the battle against child sexual abuse, successful speaking programs were exhilarating.

One early summer day, as I waited to take the podium before my hometown Women's Club, my thoughts drifted back to when I first moved to New Hampshire six years earlier. Back then, because of my fear of public speaking, I asked my co-chair of the Luncheon Group to give our monthly report at their general meeting. Today I was about to be their featured speaker, but remembering how well prepared I was, a calmness enveloped me. That calmness lingered during my presentation when I observed the audience's attentive faces as they listened to what I had to say. Later, the Program Chair said the record-breaking attendance proved that members were eager to have some meetings that addressed serious issues. For me, that victory was a personal milestone.

That night, when Dick called the crusty New Hampshire farmer who cut our hay field, his wife answered. Dick said she blurted out, "Heard your wife talk today. Hadn't been to one of them meetins' for over 20 years. She was good." Dick said she was lucky she caught a good one. She answered with the most pleasing feedback of all, "Wasn't luck. I went to hear what she talked about."

On another occasion, Sandy and I spoke to the medical staff at Dartmouth/Hitchcock Hospital in Lebanon, New Hampshire. A physician had called Rape and Assault because he wanted his staff to become better informed about child sexual abuse.

Although somewhat daunted, I admired his openness to request a speaker from a woman's crisis center. I reassured my fluttery stomach that I had valuable information they needed and wanted to hear. Once the presentation started, I easily settled into the comfort zone that I had gained from speaking to smaller medical groups throughout my area.

As usual, the question and answer period that followed made me aware of the most pressing questions that were on the audience's mind. A psychiatric nurse spoke up. "I assume that you're a social worker and that's how you got into this field."

"No. I'm not a social worker. Actually, I was a marketing major at the University of Connecticut. I started out in the field of advertising and marketing in New York City."

The nurse looked stunned. "How in the world did you get from there to here?"

I was formulating my answer when the physician who chaired the workshop took the microphone. "I'd like to answer that. If she were a social worker, she never would have become such a strong advocate for change. Social workers enforce the law. They don't break ground and take on The System. They don't become spokespeople for the cause. It's *because* she majored in marketing that she's good for this type of work. She's using all her marketing skills. She's just marketing a different product."

Now it was my turn to look stunned. I took the microphone. "I had never looked at it that way. It's true. I had to spend time in the trenches before I could understand the issue, similar to doing marketing research, and then use my skills to push my product. You're right. It's all about marketing."

Over the years, public speaking became an integral part of my job—radio, TV, panels, workshops, and community requests. I grabbed every opportunity to educate the public. Thankfully, my public speaking jitters became a thing of the past.

25   Training the Volunteers

Volunteers were the lifeblood of our agency. Without their dedicated commitment, we couldn't operate our 24-hour crisis line. However, because manning a crisis line can be both emotionally draining and time consuming, many drop out once they realize what they've gotten themselves into, so we were always in grave need of replacements. Consequently, we offered ongoing training workshops.

Prospective volunteers underwent about thirty hours of classroom training in addition to outside reading assignments. The all-day Saturday sessions were held in a conference room in our local hospital. Once the volunteers were qualified to man the crisis line, there were weekly case management meetings with the staff where everyone discussed the cases they had handled that week.

After I had gained more confidence in the public speaking arena, I agreed to present the child sexual abuse training session to our new class of potential volunteers. I had the knowledge to do it but I was scared. Deanna had always done the child sexual abuse presentations so the bar was set high, a standard that had propelled me to become a volunteer. I didn't want to let the agency down.

Deanna was such an articulate presenter that she used only the barest notes, so I had little to guide me. To prepare myself for a seven-hour day, I meticulously outlined every word I planned to say and practiced my delivery over and over. As I drove to my first training session, I shook my head when I thought about how far Rape and Assault had pushed me to expand my horizons. It had been a long journey for that prospective volunteer who had hidden in the back row hoping she wouldn't be noticed, afraid to open her mouth among the young, intimidating group of activists.

At precisely 9 a. m. on a Saturday morning, my first training session began with twenty-five potential volunteers in attendance. Fifty eager eyes waited for me to begin as I clutched my already well-worn notes.

I welcomed everyone and thanked them for coming. At least that's what I tried to do. I mouthed the words but no sound came out. I cleared my throat and coughed. I tried to apologize. Nothing. A living nightmare. A volunteer rushed out and got me a drink of water. I gulped it down with a desert thirst and then heard myself saying, "Good morning. Thank you for coming." I kept that water glass full for the rest of the day.

As the morning progressed, I loosened up. The joy of teaching what I knew was exciting. I welcomed questions along the way and found the spontaneous format comfortable. There was so much to say and I had to keep my eye on the clock to make sure I was on target to cover my ambitious agenda.

At the end of the day, I came home knowing that I had fulfilled my goal. Twenty-five potential volunteers were prepared to handle a child sexual abuse call on the crisis line, with enough understanding of the issue to assure the caller she had called the right agency before referring the calls to me or Deanna. Perhaps some would eventually handle cases on their own.

That was the first of many training sessions to follow. As I trained and observed potential volunteers, Deanna and I monitored their progress and their ability to deal with such needy victims and their families. We did that because some volunteers came to us with unresolved issues of their own and were too fragile to handle these cases effectively.

One day, a potential volunteer handed me a note during the lunch break saying that I was a reincarnation of Jesus Christ and bestowing unrealistic blessings on me. I set up a private appointment with her at which time she poured out her own tragic story. I gently guided her into therapy, stressing how her caring concern could help others once she healed from her own wounds. She thanked me and said she would volunteer for her church in other areas while undergoing therapy.

Other times, potential problems didn't show up until after a volunteer had successfully manned the crisis line and we felt she was ready to handle child sexual abuse cases. One such case resulted from a call I received from a victim who had called our crisis line and was put in touch with that volunteer. The victim never received a follow-up call as promised. When I reached our volunteer by phone, she acknowledged that she had been too personally traumatized by the case history and hadn't called anyone or gotten out of bed for two days. I arranged for her to come to our office so we could discuss the situation further. When we explored her feelings, she understood why she could no longer man the crisis line. However, she continued to contribute to Rape and Assault in numerous other ways and became an invaluable member of our team.

I always looked forward to the training programs, remembering how life altering my own experience had been. I always hoped for a potential volunteer who could handle cases independently.

26 Three-Year-Old on Trial

I sat frozen in my chair, my hand tightly gripping the phone. A young, divorced mother, Cindy, was telling me that her three-year-old daughter, Sarah, told her that daddy had tickled her pee-pee when she visited him. Cindy's voice rose in anguish: "It's just like that bastard to do something like that to get back at me for leaving him. That's the last he's going to see our kid. Can you please talk to Sarah to see if she tells you the same story?"

This was the *first* time Sarah told her story.

My mind raced. How do I talk to a three-year-old about alleged sexual touching? Should I tell the mother I am not qualified to work with such a young child? Or should I maintain a false confidence to support her? If sexual abuse is disclosed, how can such a young child go through a criminal justice system designed for adults? How can I do nothing when a mother believes her child is in danger?

I set up an appointment to meet with them the following morning. Cindy had given me permission to use our large, anatomically correct, handmade cloth dolls when I spoke with Sarah. My mind raced. Three-year-olds had to be protected. But how?

To refresh my knowledge, I browsed through a book on child development from our reference library and learned that three-year-olds were described in terms of *Goodbye Babyhood—Hello Childhood*. They can be reasoned with; 80% of their words are understandable; they talk in complete sentences of 3-5 words; they listen attentively, accept suggestions, and follow simple directions. They enjoy making others laugh, being silly, and are losing shyness toward strangers.

I decided to process this case the same way I would with an older child. However, what I would do differently was that I would document every step it took to protect a three-year-old from an alleged perpetrator, under the current New Hampshire criminal justice system to see where the case took me. How soon would it inevitably break down?

The following morning Cindy, Sarah and I arrived at our office and we introduced ourselves. Cindy was a young, attractive brunette who spoke with conviction. Sarah, an adorable, blonde, curly top, was outgoing and we conversed easily.

However, Sarah clung onto Cindy when we asked her if she would go into a room with me alone. Cindy softly but firmly reminded her daughter of their conversation at home. Sarah reluctantly accompanied me after Cindy assured her that she would be sitting right where she was and Sarah could come out at any time to check that she was still there. Cindy kept a level, natural voice, without baby talk, that assumed Sarah would do as she was told.

When Sarah and I were alone, I thanked her for coming in to talk to me. We chatted about everyday things. Sarah was bright and alert. I got her talking about herself, and she reveled in being the center of attention. In some ways, it was easier establishing a rapport with her than with older children who had developed defenses. She had a trusting innocence that was endearing.

When she seemed relaxed, I pulled out our soft, fully-clothed, anatomically-correct dolls. I suggested we play a game with them—the girl doll could be Sarah and the man doll could be her daddy. She could use the dolls to show and tell me what she and daddy did when she visited him. She was eager to do it.

Using the dolls, Sarah began the day when her daddy picked her up. She enjoyed using the dolls to act out everything she and daddy did during the day. She said she liked visiting her daddy. I expressed great interest in everything she said, saying she was lucky to have a daddy who did fun things with her.

When we got to the part where she and daddy were at his house and they snuggled together, it was surprisingly easy to get her to talk about it. She casually took the man doll's pants off and giggled when she saw his penis. Then she undressed the girl doll. Sarah was very curious to see the doll's pee-pee area and wanted to know if hers looked like that. When I said yes, she stared and felt it with her fingers.

After awhile, I gently reminded her to use the dolls to show me what she and daddy did when she was at his house. She casually acted out the alleged sexual abuse, mostly touching and rubbing of her sexual parts. She said it felt good. She demonstrated how he gave her hugs and kisses too and she liked that. Such innocence. However, for the sake of objectivity, I stayed outwardly calm as she spoke, with minimum change of expression or voice.

This was the *second* time Sarah told her story.

When Sarah and I were finished talking, we rejoined Cindy. Sarah, in great spirits, ran over to her and giggled about the doll I had with a pee-pee. I asked Sarah if mommy could have a turn to talk with me and she quickly agreed. When I gave her a bucket of toys to play with, she asked if she could play with my dolls and I gave them to her.

I told Cindy what Sarah had alleged. Through angry tears, she vowed to make her ex-husband pay for what he did. There would be no more visitations, even if she had to run away with Sarah.

We discussed Cindy's options—reporting it to the Department of Children and Youth Services (DCYS) and having a social worker investigate the case or going to the police station and having Sarah tell her story to a detective. She chose the latter because she wanted her ex-husband to know she meant business and would use every means at her disposal to keep him from seeing Sarah again. She thought a detective would scare him more than a social worker.

Accordingly, I called the police station in the town where the alleged abuse occurred. The call was directed to Chief Karl. He said that this was their first child sexual abuse case and that he would handle it himself. I filled him in with some background information. He asked me to bring our anatomically correct dolls with me when I accompanied mother and daughter to the police station. I offered to be in the room with him when he spoke with Sarah; he welcomed my presence.

Meanwhile, Cindy also stayed calm and gave no indication to Sarah about her concerns. When the three of us walked into the police station, Sarah was excited "to see where the policemen lived." Chief Karl, a 40ish, tall, slender man with warm eyes, greeted us at the door and we introduced ourselves.

Once again, Cindy told Sarah she would wait there while the three of us went into another room. When Sarah hesitated, Cindy stared at her and didn't say anything, assuming that Sarah would do as she asked. Sarah finally took my hand and the three of us walked into a large room down the hall.

Chief Karl took immediate control of the situation. He asked her lots of questions about herself and let her babble on. Once again, she loved being the center of attention. Then he casually picked up the dolls and said he would like to hear about what she and daddy did when she visited him. She eagerly used the dolls to give him a detailed run-through of her fun day with daddy. Chief Karl's animated response to everything she told him encouraged Sarah to continue. He said he enjoyed hearing about all the fun things she and her daddy did together.

When they eventually reached the point where the alleged sexual abuse took place, Sarah lowered her head and didn't say anything, more hesitant than when she was with me. She looked up at me with a questioning look. I told her she was doing well and that Chief Karl was her friend. She stared at the floor in silence. Chief Karl had put some toys on the floor before we had arrived and Sarah got off her chair, sat on the floor, and started to play with them. Chief Karl joined her on the floor and they put a pre-school puzzle together.

Then Chief Karl picked up the dolls and brought her back to where they were earlier; Sarah lost eye contact with him and crawled under a table. By scrunching himself down, he joined her under the table. She seemed to feel safer there and used the dolls to show what she and daddy did, describing the alleged sexual abuse.

This was the *third* time Sarah told her story.

I felt a sense of relief after Sarah told her story to Chief Karl because that meant the case was officially in the hands of The System and I could now observe how it played out. Chief Karl would do an investigation and determine if he thought a crime had been committed. I would set up counseling for Sarah; a three-year-old needed a professional to evaluate her and to then be her voice.

Cindy's immediate priority was to have visitations with the father stopped. Since The Division of Children and Youth Services (DCYS) held the legal authority to investigate such cases, Cindy asked that I call them. By law, Chief Karl was also required by law to do this.

When I called DCYS, the social worker asked why I hadn't called them first, as the law mandated, instead of talking to the child myself and then taking her to the police station. I explained that Cindy wanted Sarah to talk to an outsider first in order to corroborate Sarah's story before getting involved in The System. I further explained that after Sarah disclosed the alleged abuse to me, Cindy chose to contact the police first (a parent's right) because she felt that someone from law enforcement would put a bigger scare into her husband. After our phone call, a social worker interviewed Sarah and conducted an Intake and Assessment Evaluation to see if she felt the child was in any immediate danger.

This was the *fourth* time Sarah told her story.

At this point, the child protective acts came into play.

CHAPTER 169-C, CHILD PROTECTION ACT OF
NEW HAMPSHIRE

*Outsiders cannot be privy to any further information on the
case.*

169-C:14 CHILD PROTECTION ACT: HEARINGS
NOT OPEN TO THE PUBLIC.

*The general public shall be excluded from any hearing
under this chapter and such hearings shall, whenever
possible, not be held in criminal trials. Only such persons
as the parties, their witnesses, counsel and representatives of
the agencies present to perform their official duties shall be
admitted, except that other persons invited by a party may
attend, with the court's prior approval.*

169-C:15 PRELIMINARY HEARING:

*A preliminary hearing shall be conducted by the court to
determine if reasonable cause exists to believe that the child
is being abused or neglected.*

When the Preliminary Hearing was held, Cindy's attorney asked
me to testify. He led me to a small room with a table and chairs
that sat about ten people. Among those in attendance were
Cindy, the DCYS social worker, lawyers from both sides, and the
defendant who was seated directly opposite me. The judge
entered and sat at the head of the table, alongside my seat. He
introduced himself and asked each of us to do the same.

The defendant's lawyer tried to have me evicted as a non-
professional, under the confidentiality clause. The judge asked me
who I was, what my credentials were, and how I got involved in
the case. I gave him a brief summary. He seemed interested in
hearing about Rape and Assault's work with child sexual abuse

victims and asked intelligent questions. He then said he wanted to hear what I had to say.

The judge had me go first so I could leave after my testimony, thereby adhering to the confidentiality clause. I stayed surprisingly calm when the judge sat back in his chair, folded his hands on the table, and asked me to tell him everything about my conversation with Sarah and what she had alleged. I rose above my nerves because I wanted my voice heard. I detailed what had transpired, starting from the minute Sarah walked into our office. I surprised myself at how much I wanted to observe the defendant's reaction when confronted with Sarah's allegations. I looked him in the eye when I voiced what Sarah had told me, alleging sexual abuse. He glared back with icy eyes, stony faced.

After I finished, the judge sat up in his chair, unfolded his hands, and said "Hmmm," as he continued to stare at me. He finally thanked me for my testimony and said I could leave.

The judge later ruled that the father would have court-ordered, supervised visitations until a final custody hearing could be held. Cindy was upset that he still had any visitation rights but I was comfortable with the judge's decision. It's hard to take away a father's rights on just the say-so of a three-year-old. A judge has to consider every possibility. Could a mother have prompted her three-year-old to say that, to get back at her ex? Could the story be part of a three-year-old's fantasy world? It can be a tough call.

The next step in the process was an Adjudicatory Hearing where a final ruling would be handed down:

169-C:18 ADJUDICATORY HEARING:

An adjudicatory hearing shall be conducted by the court separate from the trial of criminal cases. The petitioner shall present witnesses to testify in support of the petition and any other evidence necessary to support the petition, in this case to Revoke the Father's Visitation Rights. The petitioners shall have the right to present evidence and witnesses on their own behalf and to cross-examine adverse witnesses.

The date of the Adjudicatory Hearing conflicted with a business/pleasure trip I was scheduled to take with Dick. Although the confidentiality clause prohibited me from being in the courtroom, I felt that my presence was necessary at such a landmark point, in case the judge called me in to testify. Therefore, Dick kindly picked me up at the airport two days later.

On the day of the hearing, all the professionals involved in the case were present. I had arranged for Sarah to see a leading clinical psychologist in the field of child sexual abuse and they had had many productive sessions. A three-year-old needed the validation of a credible therapist who could evaluate her allegations; the court relied heavily on therapists' recommendations. Police Chief Karl would also testify.

When the court was called into session, I anxiously waited in the lounge. Above all, I wanted Sarah to have a fair hearing. After about an hour, the therapist exited the courtroom. They had allowed her to testify first because being away from her practice was costing her money. Her face flushed, she said she was pleased with how her testimony went.

After about two hours, the judge called a recess. I was told that my name had come up because I had taken the child's initial testimony. When the defense attorney sarcastically tried to discredit my non-professional background, the judge ordered him to stop the sarcasm.

When the testimonies were concluded, the judge took the case under advisement. He eventually ruled that the father would continue to have court-supervised visitations until the court revisited the case in three months.

Meanwhile, Chief Karl decided there was enough evidence to send the case up to the County Attorney's Office (CAO). An

Assistant County Attorney questioned Sarah to assess her credibility.

This was the *fifth* time Sarah told her story.

When Prosecutor X decided there was sufficient evidence to press criminal charges, Sarah would become the youngest child to enter the criminal justice system in the state of New Hampshire.

Because the wheels of justice grind slowly, Sarah had turned four years old by the time she had to testify in front of a Grand Jury.

GRAND JURY

A Grand Jury determines whether or not there is enough evidence for a trial by examining the evidence presented to them by a prosecutor. With sufficient evidence, the Grand Jury issues an indictment. It is traditionally larger than a petit jury which is used during a trial.

The day before Sarah was scheduled to testify, she stated that she would only tell her story to those people about what she and daddy did together if she could sit on my lap. Concern flooded me. Was all this too much to expect of such a young child? As this would be my first appearance before a Grand Jury, I had no idea what happened during those confidential sessions or what Sarah would be faced with.

On the day of her scheduled testimony, we arrived promptly at 9 a. m. as scheduled. However, because of delays, it was five hours before Sarah was called. Without a nap, she was understandably tired and cranky. *Ludicrous.* How could anyone put a four-year-old who was supposed to be a victim through this kind of punishment?

We finally entered the Grand Jury room. The jurors looked relaxed, sitting in scattered chairs. Their expressions softened when they spotted this scared, four-year-old cutie holding on to my hand for dear life.

Sarah looked terrified and, when we sat down, she quickly snuggled in my lap and buried her head in my chest. As they had rehearsed, Prosecutor X started out asking her easy, general questions to establish her credibility and show that she knew how important it was to tell the truth. Sarah wormed her way deeper in my lap as the questions proceeded and never looked at him, but answered his questions. When it came to the part where she and daddy snuggled together, he asked her what happened next. Her body tensed against mine and she looked up at me. I softly encouraged her to tell them what she and daddy did.

This was the *sixth* time Sarah told her story.

When Sarah's testimony was over, she asked me to carry her out. She was exhausted. Later on, her therapist and Chief Karl would testify about her allegations, in greater detail.

When Sarah's father was eventually indicted, I granted an interview with an Associated Press reporter. Without identifying the child's identity, I handed him my log depicting all the steps a three-year-old who alleges child sexual abuse has to go through, under the current New Hampshire Criminal Justice System. I passed no judgment on the guilt or innocence of the alleged perpetrator. My mission was to point out that there was a crucial need to make changes in how The System accommodates young children alleging sexual abuse. Because the log was printed in its entirety in the leading New Hampshire newspapers, I was heartened that the public was now aware of the severity of the problem.

Meanwhile, Cindy's goal never wavered—to keep Sarah away from her father. Since she wanted to spare Sarah the trauma of testifying against the daddy she still loved, Cindy told her ex that if he gave up his visitation rights, she would defer the criminal case. He agreed.

Cindy and Sarah moved out of state and started a new life.

Deanna and I concluded that cases involving children under six years old were almost impossible to prove in a criminal court of law. How could Sarah have undergone being depositioned by a defense attorney who had free rein to ask anything he wanted, with no supervision? Or have taken the stand and testified against the daddy she loved? Or withstood a rigorous cross examination by an aggressive defense attorney? How could an assistant county attorney have won the case based solely on the word of a three-year-old, with no witnesses or physical evidence?

We decided that Rape and Assault would never again take another three-year-old child to the police department with the possibility of initiating a criminal investigation. When our forefathers wrote the laws, they simply didn't foresee that such a System would be applied to the youngest of minors.

However, Deanna and I were left with a daunting question. How do you ensure both a child's safety and an alleged perpetrator's rights? One more pressing issue to be added to Rape and Assault's fast growing agenda.

27 Adult Survivors

My first inkling that something new was amiss came from several mothers of the sexually abused children for whom I had advocated. Because I was sensitive to their fragile state once they realized that their children had been sexually abused, I always gave them ongoing help, knowing that a strong, supportive mother was crucial to her child's recovery.

I soon came to realize that, regardless of whether their child's perpetrator was inside or outside the family, a surprising number of mothers threw out confusing hints during our talks such as, "I can *feel* what my child is going through." They would often offer clues to test my reaction and, once they felt safe enough to trust me, they disclosed that they, too, were sexually abused as children. When they saw the care I gave to their children, I sensed that they also yearned for that same level of nurturing. As more of them opened up to me, it soon became clear that, even after many years, these adult survivors of child sexual abuse were walking around with open wounds.

As the media continued to uncover and expose the stark reality of child sexual abuse, Rape and Assault began to receive impassioned calls from other adult survivors. At first, Deanna and I didn't know how to help them. Their abuses were well past the current Statue of Limitations so they could not pursue criminal action. We also realized that we had to educate ourselves about the dynamics involved in being an adult survivor before we could counsel them. Even though scant material was available on the subject, I managed to find a couple of good books and gained some much-needed understanding of this group of victims.

I learned that adult survivors of child sexual abuse needed a caring listener who empathized with their pain and gave them permission to allow their tears to flow. They needed to be reminded that, in the days when their abuse occurred, child sexual abuse was a well-kept secret, that children have been molested since the dawn of time. In addition, before the women's movement smashed down those walls of secrecy, there were few advocates who spoke out about this horrible, unthinkable crime.

These adult survivors needed the same validation as the children I counseled. They needed to know that the abuse wasn't their fault and they shouldn't harbor feelings of guilt or shame. They needed confirmation that they had been naive children when threatened with awful things that would happen if they told— such as their beloved dog being poisoned—and of course they believed it; that any youngster could be persuaded that nobody would believe a child over an adult; that it wasn't their fault if they told someone and weren't believed, or perhaps even punished for having such disgusting thoughts, or, worse yet, accused of causing the abuse.

Adult survivors needed to remember that children are spontaneous, loving, and trusting, expecting the adults in charge to love them back appropriately. Because over 85% of child sexual abuse victims know their perpetrator, chances are they were betrayed by those they loved, trusted, or were told to obey.

Since most survivors are not aware of the long-lasting effects of their abuse, it is imperative they not underestimate the power it has over their lives, how it can control them twenty, thirty, or even forty years later. Many do not associate their feelings of anger with their child sexual abuse because the confusion, betrayal, and fear overshadow the injustices and shame.

Because adult survivors who reveal their abuse for the first time are in a perilous state, I stressed the importance of therapy in order to deal with the overwhelming feelings that would probably emerge. The time had come to put the victimized child in a proper emotional place where she could finally be nurtured and loved and told she was never at fault for an adult's misconduct.

In order to find the right therapist for each survivor, I did research and found the most qualified therapists with expertise in the field, a select few whom I came to know well. They were among the finest people I have ever met—kind, firm, and caring.

My toughest task was finding ways that victims could afford therapy. Those with qualifying health insurance could choose their therapist. For those without coverage, I had to locate qualified community resources that took clients on a sliding scale. For those on Medicaid, I had to find therapists who would accept the low rate Medicaid paid. It was a maddening battle that demanded top priority and hours of my precious time.

RITA

As time went on and more resources became available, I checked on whether there were support groups for adult victims of child sexual abuse. I came across some survivors who had formed their own group. I called their number, told the volunteer who answered who I was, and asked if I could possibly attend a couple of their sessions to educate myself and to see if I felt comfortable referring clients to them. At first, she hesitated. For privacy reasons, no outsiders were allowed to sit in on their meetings. After we spoke further and I described what my work entailed, she relented and said I could come.

On the night of the meeting, I quietly entered the room. About ten ordinary looking women were sitting in a circle. The person I spoke with on the phone greeted me and asked me to join them. After she introduced me to the group, she asked me to explain what my job was and why I would like to attend their meeting. After that, they would decide whether they were comfortable with my staying. When I finished speaking, I was grateful when they said I could remain.

The meeting began with each member, who chose to, talking about her week, focusing on her feelings and how she dealt with them. I sat there mesmerized. I had never been exposed to such raw honesty. Here were women who felt safe enough with each other to share their most intimate feelings and then receive the comfort, understanding, and honest feedback of friends. It was powerful.

That segment took up most of the meeting. Before they concluded, they invited anyone to speak who might have a special need. A new member, Rita, who had not previously spoken, slowly raised her hand. She looked to be in her thirties. Her heavy-set frame was covered by a man's huge black and white checkered flannel shirt that came down almost to her knees.

In a gruff voice, Rita blurted out that she had been sexually abused by her father and had never told anyone. After a tense silence, someone asked if this was something she would like to share with the group. Dead silence. Then someone else suggested that she might want to tell them just a little bit—how much was up to her.

With downcast eyes, Rita said it began when she was five years old, just after she started kindergarten, after her mother went back to work. Another member in the group quietly interjected that she could empathize because she had a somewhat similar experience.

Sometimes Rita wouldn't speak for a long time but nobody broke the silence. She eventually gave out other bits of information. Her father had intercourse with her until she ran away from home when she was sixteen. The whole time she spoke, Rita never exhibited any emotion or shed a tear. She finally said she didn't want to talk any more.

Other members spoke out with genuine support. Because they had all shared similar pain, there was no need for any windbag sentiments. I thought that Rita *had* to know their concerns were genuine. They said she could call any of them during the week if she felt the need to talk.

When the meeting concluded, I was wiped out from being privy to such bleeding emotions. I could only imagine the depths of their feelings.

When I returned for the next meeting, I hoped to hear more from Rita. The last one to arrive, she strode in with a somber face, head hung low, and took the last seat next to mine, without saying a word. When the meeting started, the facilitator asked Rita if she would like to begin this week sharing what kind of week she had and what feelings might have emerged.

Rita sat there for a long time without responding. When she finally spoke, she just about knocked me off my chair. She pounded her fists on the bottom of her chair and shouted that she was furious with all of them because they had weakened her into telling them about her abuse. She had vowed she would never tell anyone. I had never seen such killing anger on anyone's face. She kept slamming her fist into her hand. Her out-of-control anger, contorted face, and inflammatory eyes scared me. Would she turn violent? Then, without another word, she grabbed her bag and stormed out of the room.

At first, everyone just sat there immobilized, immersed in their own thoughts. Gradually, they opened up a dialogue about repressed anger, questioning whether any one else had dealt with that level of anger the first time they revealed their sexual abuse.

This group of women didn't spin their wheels in self-pity. They faced the issue head-on and wanted to grow from this experience, hoping to help Rita if she returned. They each agreed to research material on that level of repressed anger and bring their information to the group the following week.

I sat there in shock from having witnessed such raw, explosive anger. Given that these women were victims of the ultimate betrayal of trust when they were innocent children and robbed of their childhood, I could understand Rita's rage. We are innocent for a short period of time and the experience of childhood trust is irreplaceable. Although Rita might never return, the members weren't discouraged; perhaps she wasn't ready at this time. She knew the door was always open.

My sessions with that support group and those remarkable women gave me a richer understanding of adult survivors, made me a stronger advocate, and enabled me to refer several clients to them, with excellent feedback. I went on to become a vocal advocate of the therapeutic value of qualified support groups.

28 No Room at the Inn

I live in a scenic New Hampshire village blessed with open spaces, apple orchards, farm land, two-acre zoning, and a typical New England town square. While I was exposed to the seedy side of life at Rape and Assault, the rural, pastoral setting of the country roads and the comforting arms of our saltbox house at the edge of a pine forest nurtured my soul.

My village has few, if any, homeless people. That's why I was surprised to get a phone call from a local resident begging me to help an eighteen-year-old homeless girl named Jean, from a neighboring town, whom she had befriended. Jean's family had kicked her out while she was still in high school and my caller was outraged that an eighteen-year-old high school student had to live on the street. I arranged a time for her to drop Jean off at our office. I would listen to her story and see what resources were available to help her out.

That afternoon, a downtrodden teenager entered our office. Jean was short and chubby, her face void of all emotions. Her stringy, brown hair fell below her shoulders, with bangs that almost covered her eyes. She wore a long sleeve, striped cotton shirt, frayed dungarees and a dirty black windbreaker. Her once-white sneakers were now a grimy grey. Other than a darting glance or two, she stared at the floor.

After we entered a private room, I introduced myself and told her briefly about the work I did for Rape and Assault. I asked her to verify that she had been kicked out of her house and had no money, food, or place to live. With eyes still downcast, she nodded.

Because Jean had yet to look at me or say a word, I continued to initiate the conversation.

"Is it okay with you if I ask you some personal questions about your situation so I can figure out the best way to help you?"

Jean shrugged her shoulders, and then nodded her head.

"Thank you. How old are you?"

"Eighteen."

"How long have you been homeless?"

"About two weeks."

"That's a long time to be without a place to sleep or food to eat. Where do you sleep?"

"In the woods."

"How do you get food to eat?"

"I steal food."

"You have to eat to stay alive."

Jean nodded her head.

"Do you have any family that could help you out?"

"No."

"You are a high school student?"

Jean nodded.

"How long have you attended your high school?"

"Since I moved in with my father. About a year."

"Have you attended any classes these past two weeks?"

"No. I can't get there."

"Where did you live before you moved in with your father a year ago?"

"In a home for teens with no other place to live."

"How long did you live there?"

"About four years."

"Where did you live before that?"

"In an orphanage."

"How long did you live in the orphanage?"

"Since I was six years old."

"Why were you living in an orphanage?"

"My father couldn't take care of my sister and me by himself."

"Where was your mother?"

Jean spoke her longest sentence, in a lifeless voice.

"She left home when I was six years old and never came back. She couldn't take care of us. I don't know where she went."

"Did you ever hear from her again?"

"No."

"How do you feel about that?"

Jean raised her head and glanced at me for the first time. In a defiant tone, she snapped, "I don't care! Like my father said, 'She was garbage we were glad to be rid of.' "

"Did you live with your father after your mother left?"

"For a couple of months. Then he took me and my sister to the orphanage."

"How do you feel about that?"

"Okay. He had to work."

"How did you like living at the orphanage?"

"It was okay. I had my sister."

"Did your father visit you?"

"Once in a while. Then he got busy, and didn't come anymore. Even at Christmas."

"How did you feel about that?"

"It was okay. I took care of my sister."

"How old were you when you left the orphanage?"

"Thirteen. They don't let teenagers live there after that—they're too much trouble."

"Where did you go then?"

"To a home for teenagers."

"How did you like living there?"

"It was noisy. I didn't know nobody. I wasn't so lonely when my sister came a year later."

"How long did you live there?"

"Until I was seventeen."

"Where did you go then?"

"My father came to get me. He said he was married again, that my stepmother's name was Ann. He wanted to see how it worked out if I lived with them."

"Is this something you wanted to do?"

"I felt bad about leavin' my sister, but she had more friends than I did. She said it was okay. I wanted to live in a home with my father."

"How did that work out?"

"Okay at first. It was nice and quiet. It was hard finding stuff to talk about when we had supper. They said I was very quiet, and I said that's the way I was. They asked if I was sad, and I said 'sometimes'. They kept askin' me if I liked livin' there and I said 'yes.'"

"How did you like Ann?"

"She was nice to me. My father was nice too. My favorite time of day was after supper when Ann and I finished the dishes and all of us watched TV until bedtime. I liked the shows they watched, and we didn't have to think about what to talk about."

"What was your favorite show?"

"Bonanza."

"That was one of my favorite shows too—they were such a caring family."

"Yea. I like the father."

"Me too. Did you start high school when you moved in with your father?"

"Uh huh. Ann brought me there and signed me up. I was in the 11th Grade."

"Did you like it there?"

"No. Nobody spoke to me. I didn't have any friends. The boys laughed at me and called me Tubby."

"Sometimes it's hard to make friends in high school when you're new. And some boys can be mean at that age. I'm sorry you had to go through that. I hope you get a chance to go back and finish high school."

"I don't care if I finish. I was failin' most subjects anyway. The guidance counselor said I could think about getting my GED."

"I hope you do. A high school diploma is important when you're looking for a job."

Jean shrugged her shoulders.

"So, let's see. We left off when you were living with your Dad and Ann. You said they were nice to you. I'm wondering why they kicked you out. Is this something you would like to talk about?"

Jean was quiet for a long time. Then she took a couple of deep sighs.

"I don't know."

"Maybe you could tell me a little bit and see how it goes from there."

Another long, silent pause.

"My father turned out to be…not so nice."

"I'm sad to hear that."

"Well, I should of knowed better than to get my hopes up. It was my own stupid fault."

"It's hard not to wish for good things to happen. Especially for someone like you who's had so many sad things happen in your life."

"Well, he turned out to be a fuckin' bastard."

"Those are strong words. I'm wondering what he did to make you so angry."

"It's disgustin'."

"Jean, I've worked with abused children for eight years. I do it because my heart aches for them and I know anything disgusting that an adult does to a child is never the child's fault. It's *always* the fault of the adult who did something to them. I promise you that nothing you say will make me think less of you."

"Have you worked with kids whose fathers had sex with them?"

"Lots of them."

Long silence.

"My father fucked me."

"Jean, I am so sorry to hear you say that. That is one of the worst things a father can do to a daughter."

"Yea! He said if I told anyone, nobody would believe a liar like me. That I would be sent back to the house I was livin' in before. I hated it there. A guy that worked there fucked me since I was fourteen. So I figured I might as well live in a real home. My father only did it when he was drunk and when Ann wasn't home so it wasn't that he did it all the time. So I kept my mouth shut and closed my eyes when he did it. It didn't take him long."

"It sounds as though you were caught between two bad choices."

"Yup."

"Jean, do you understand that what happened wasn't your fault, that it was nothing you wanted to happen?"

"Maybe if I just told him to cut it out he would of. I just laid there and let him do it."

"Remember—you were caught between two terrible men. They were cruel cowards—taking advantage of a terrified teenager who had no other place to go."

"Yea. I hated it when they fucked me. Especially my father. With his baloney that he had me move in with him so he could make up for all the time he didn't take care of me. All he wanted was someone to fuck."

"I'm glad to see you getting angry. Hold onto that anger for now—use that energy to help you fight back and get back on your feet."

"Yea."

"Jean, I'm still wondering why they kicked you out of the house. Are you comfortable talking about that?"

"Umm—Yea—Why not? I *wanna* tell you. It happened one night when Ann was out bowlin' and my father was finishin' a six-pack of beer and had fallen asleep in front of the TV. I was tired so I went to bed. I slept on the pull-out couch in the livin' room. The next thing I knew, there he was. He had already pulled out his cock and was pullin' down my bottom. He was on top of me when in walked Ann. She screamed then ran into their bedroom and slammed the door. My father jumped up, slapped my face, and called me a dirty cunt. He pulled up his pants and ran into the bedroom.

"Then my father and Ann screamed at each other for a long time. Then their voices got lower, and I couldn't hear what they were saying. Then it was quiet. Then the next morning my father told me to pack my bags and get the hell out. He said I was a no-good troublemaker and that I could end up in the gutter just like my mother for all he cared. So that was it. I left."

When Jean finished telling me her story, we were both spent. I gently brought up her feelings about all that had happened to her but she was non-committal, devoid of feeling, depressed. Thanking her for sharing it with me, I promised to find help for her. I gave her lunch money and told her I would check out what help was out there. I gave her a book entitled, Daugherty: *Why Me?*, a simple, nurturing book we kept in stock for someone who has just disclosed sexual abuse.

Since Jean was still a high school student, my first call was to the Division of Children and Youth Services where I spoke with a social worker.

"I'm working with a high school student who was kicked out of her home, has no money and lives on the street."

"That's horrible. Please give me the essential facts and we will get in touch with her. What's her name?"

"Jean Morley."

"Age?"

"Eighteen."

"Eighteen! She's not a minor!"

"I know. But she's a student. A high school senior with no place to live."

"I understand and sympathize. But the law states that we can only serve minors under eighteen years of age. I have no other choice."

"Who do I turn to then?"

"I suggest you call the state offices of the Division of Health & Human Services."

I immediately called and gave them the details.

"I can empathize, Ms. Bonati. I really can. But, legally, she is an adult and not entitled to the benefits she had as a minor. At eighteen years old, she will have to find a job and support herself. She can also check into going on welfare."

"But she's still a high school student with no place to live. She needs a place to sleep *tonight*! And food to eat *now*. How can she work full-time and still finish high school?"

"It's sad. But that's how the law reads. My hands are tied."

After that shocker, every other avenue I tried was a dead end. At eighteen years old, you're on your own.

Frustrated, I joined Jean who had come back to our office. I spelled out what she was up against.

"I'm really sorry but I've tried everything to get you immediate financial support but once you're eighteen, you are no longer entitled to the benefits you got as a minor."

"I don't wanna go back to high school anyway. I'll get a job."

"Unfortunately, that might be your best choice for right now. We do have a shelter for battered and sexually abused women. Because you are eighteen years old, you can stay there, free of charge, until we check on the welfare benefits you are eligible for, and you can save up enough money to live on your own."

Her whole body sagged with relief. "Wow. Thanks. Phew! That's a *big* help."

"I'll drive you there, and we'll get you settled in."

"Wow. Thanks."

Our shelter is a pleasant home in a safe neighborhood with a full-time Shelter Manager. When Rape and Assault was finally able to finance a home of its own, staff members and volunteers worked feverishly to make it inviting and comfortable. It was furnished primarily with donated or secondhand furniture and appliances. To give it a homespun look, we bought fresh linens, bedspreads, and crisp, clean curtains and painted the walls soft, pastel colors. Necessary supplies, a well-stocked refrigerator and pantry, and racks of clothing in a spacious attic are provided, free, as most clients come in with just what they have on. The night before our shelter opened, the staff and volunteers had a celebratory housewarming party joined by invited members of several police departments, the only ones who knew its location.

Jean and I arrived at our shelter about 6 p.m. I got her set up in a double room that she would share with one other person and we made up her bed. Then I gave her a tour and went over the strict rules that ensure a clean, safe, nurturing environment. She kept saying the place was so much nicer than she thought it would be. "It's the nicest house I have ever lived in."

I didn't rush her into finding a job. She needed time to catch up on her lost sleep and recover from her trauma. She eventually got a job on the night shift at a Mini-Market, earning minimum wage. After several weeks, Jean was fired for stealing, but no charges were filed, and she immediately found a job on the night shift of another gas-station Mini-Market.

 Since Jean had free room and board at our shelter, she saved her money, and after a month found an inexpensive, shared room in a downtown apartment, with three other girls ranging in ages from eighteen to twenty-four. She was on a bus route but often walked to work to save money. Although she never complained, she continued to speak in a monotone, depressed tone of voice, with little enthusiasm for anything.

After she settled in and became stronger, we talked about her father's sexual abuse.

"How are you feeling now about your father sexually abusing you?"

"I wish I could pay him back for what he did. But there's nothin' I can do."

"What he did is a criminal act and you could press charges. If found guilty, he could go to jail. But, I have to warn you. It's a long, difficult, and often an impossible case to prove in a court of law, especially if it's just one person's word against another."

"What would I have to do?"

"You'd have to go down to the police department and tell your story to a detective. I would go with you if you wanted me to. After that, the detective would conduct an investigation. He would question your father and Ann and check on your background. Chances are he would make you take a lie detector test. Then he would decide whether he thought there was enough evidence to press charges. If so, he would send the case up to the County Attorney's Office and they would call you in to talk to you. Then they would decide if there was enough evidence to bring your father to trial."

"Wow. I never thought about doin' that. I can really do that?"

"Yes. This is a decision that only you can make. Take your time. Think about it. If you do decide to go that route, we can talk about it some more. Then, after that, if you still decide to do it, I would be there to support you."

"Wow."

Jean called me early the next morning.

"Millie—I stayed awake all night thinkin' about what you said. I wanna go to the police station and talk to that detective. I'm not afraid of a lie detector test because I'm telling the truth. I want to see if a detective will arrest my father. Wouldn't *he* be shocked that mousy *me* did somethin' like that!"

"Yes he would. Come on over and I'll tell you about all the steps you'd have to take to go through with it. After that, you can decide for sure."

"Okay. But Millie—I *really* wanna do this."

A short while later, Jean and I had a long talk discussing the whole process from start to finish if she chose to file charges. We hashed over the pros and cons. It was a huge question mark whether Ann would testify on her behalf—so it could come down to Jean's word against her father's—a tough case to prove beyond a reasonable doubt. However, Jean was not deterred.

"I wanna go for it. What have I got to lose?"

"Okay. Let's do it."

I called the police department, spoke with the detective on duty, gave him the basic facts, and he said to come right in.

Jean arrived at the police station in the same outfit she wore the first time she walked into Rape and Assault—cotton shirt, worn-out dungarees and her ever-faithful black windbreaker, zipped up. Although we had other clothes at the shelter she could have worn, I wondered if she felt comfortable in that outfit because it covered up her body, which was common for sexually abused victims. Jean told me later that she thought it was her lucky outfit because she had worn it when she met me at Rape and Assault. I gave her an impulsive hug.

Jean had made great strides in looking at me when we spoke, but when we entered the police department, she stayed close and hung her head when the detective met us in the lobby, introduced himself, and took us to a private room.

When we were settled in, I sat there silently, letting the detective do his job. Once again, I was impressed with the caliber of the detective's inquisition—respectful, kind, and patient while, at the same time, asking the tough questions that were part of his investigation. As usual, the detective and I formed a close bond as we worked together to help a confused, frightened, sexually abused child.

As hard as it was for Jean to talk about this sensitive subject with a man, I admired how gutsy she was—she was determined to do it. She had to describe the nitty-gritty details of every act. After about two hours, the detective said he would arrange for her to take a lie detector test, which she passed. Even though it could not be used as evidence in a court of law, it added to her credibility. After he called Jean's father in for questioning, he would complete his investigation. He would get back to her in a week or so.

Jean called me about ten days later, panting heavily.

"The police guy just called. He told my father to come down to the police station. He said my father was shocked when he heard about what I done—that he shouted out that he was innocent and I was a liar. He said he had to kick me out because I kept stealin' money and other stuff from them after all they tried to do for me. But Millie, then the police guy said he checked into my past and was gonna send all the information up to that courthouse lawyer and let him decide what to do. Isn't it wonderful that he's gonna do that?"

"Yes it is. That means the detective felt there was enough evidence to press charges and let the County Attorney's Office look over the information and decide if there was enough evidence to go to trial."

"Oh boy! I can just see the look on my father's face when the police told him what I done. I laugh out loud every time I think about it."

I was happy for Jean that the case had been moved up to the County Attorney's Office. At the very least, her father could be held accountable for Jean's allegations. At the same time, I was also aware that this was a weak case to prove beyond a reasonable doubt. However, from here on in, it was my job to push all doubts aside and be a strong advocate for Jean, to support the decision she had made.

When the County Attorney decided to prosecute, Jean was assigned a victim-witness advocate under the Victim Advocacy Program that worked out of the County Attorney's Office.

Because Rape and Assault had a close working relationship with them, the emotional transition from me to them went smoothly. Jean worked closely with her personal advocate and would occasionally call me with the latest news during the court procedure that dragged on for months. Now that Jean had a job and a place to live, we had less contact while I became immersed in other crisis cases.

One day, when I received a call from her, her voice was shaky and she could hardly talk. "My father's lawyer wants to make a plea bargain—my father will plead guilty if I drop the charges. I don't know what to do."

"This is a big change of events. Come on in so we can talk about it."

Jean arrived at our office fearful about what to do.

"Okay Jean. This decision requires a lot of thought. We should look at the advantages of accepting or not accepting the plea."

"I think I wanna turn it down. I've dreamed so long about him goin' to jail because of what he did that I don't want him to get off free."

"I can understand how you want that and that is your right. However, why don't I point out the advantages of not going to trial and accepting his plea? That way, you can weigh both sides."

"Okay."

"You said at the beginning how important it was that everyone knew about what your father did to you—you wanted to prove that he was guilty so he couldn't call you a liar anymore."

Jean nodded her head.

"Remember how I stressed at the beginning how difficult it is for a jury to hand down a guilty verdict, beyond a reasonable doubt, when it's just one person's word against the other and there is no other evidence. Because of this, your father could be found not guilty and then he could boast that twelve jurors found him *Not Guilty*, proving that you were lying all the time."

Jean's face froze. She was quiet for a long time. I finally spoke.

"I don't want you to make up your mind about what to do right now. I want you to go home and give it a lot of thought—it's a very important decision for you."

Jean kept shaking her head. "I don't know what to do."

"Once again, think about it long and hard and call me when you want to talk about it some more."

"Okay."

Jean came in the next day and said she wanted to talk some more. "I'm drivin' myself crazy tryin' to figure out what to do. I really want to go through with it and have him hear me testify against him in court, but when I think about him maybe bein' found not guilty and then callin' me a liar, I wanna throw up."

"It's tough Jean. What would be the *worst* thing that could happen? That you wouldn't get to testify against him in court or that he would be found not guilty?"

"That he was found not guilty."

I nodded my head.

"I guess I better take his guilty plea."

"Considering everything, that's a wise decision."

When Jean left, a wave of relief swarmed through me. Although I could still applaud her for her effort if he was found not guilty, it would leave a painful hole in her heart. I was satisfied with a guilty plea that she could flaunt in his face. Later on, Jean called and said that the County Attorney's Office also thought that was a wise decision.

A couple of days later Jean called me, hysterical. She screamed into the phone. "My father changed his mind. He isn't gonna plead guilty."

Rage consumed me. I could barely get my words out.

"Come in as soon as you can so we can talk about this."

Waiting for Jean to arrive, my rage intensified. Her father's defense attorney had a reputation as a slick lawyer who did whatever it took to win a case, and he usually did. Was he deliberately playing with Jean's fragile emotions?

As an advocate, my job was to help Jean remain strong once she decided to follow through with prosecution. I had to submerge my own doubts about its possible bleak outcome. Her father's offer of a plea bargain if he admitted his guilt compelled me to force Jean to face the fact that there was a good chance that she was not going to win her case, that an admission of guilt might be her best bet. However, that realism now left Jean in a weakened state, the fight taken out of her.

When Jean arrived at our office, she looked utterly defeated.

"I'm gonna lose my case and end up with nothin'."

Even though anger and pain continued to seep through every pore of my body, I had to appear strong in order to bring back Jean's fighting spirit, the one she had before I had put the element of doubt in her mind. Although my admission of what a weak case it was loomed over us, we began the long journey of restoring Jean's confidence.

After Jean left, I called prosecutor X. He had also advised Jean to accept the guilty plea and was just as puzzled and furious about the defense attorney's motives. He was checking into whether there were any new developments that could account for this reversal.

Later on, we got a possible answer. Just prior to their offer of a plea, prosecutor X had planned to depose Ann, hoping to use her as a witness for the prosecution but now, surprisingly, Ann was listed as a witness for the defense. During Ann's deposition, she testified, under oath, that she never walked in on them having sex, that what Jean claimed never happened, that Jean was a pathological liar. It was a devastating blow.

Months of waiting for the trial to begin wore Jean down but she kept her job and hung in there.

When the case finally came to trial, I entered the courtroom thankful that the waiting was finally over as I took a seat in the front row. An anxious looking foursome were huddled together, perhaps they were friends of Jean's father. I turned around and smiled at the County Attorney's Office's trusted victim advocate sitting in the back row.

After the jury solemnly took their place in the jury box, we all rose while the judge took his seat on the bench. The day of reckoning had finally arrived.

The prosecution presented their opening arguments. They laid out a case of a father who used his child's vulnerability—a mother who deserted her at six years old; an orphanage at six years old; a teenage home for unwanted girls at thirteen years old; a father who claimed her at seventeen years old and then, like an animal, continually raped her until he was caught and threw her out; and finally, a penniless street person sleeping in the woods and stealing food to eat. "Ladies and Gentlemen of the Jury, this happened right here in the state of New Hampshire."

The defense then presented their opening arguments. They laid out a case of a child with a heartbreaking background. A mother who took off when she was six; a father who couldn't raise her alone because he had to work fulltime; a father who worried about her safety and thought she would be better taken care of in an orphanage; a father who got his life together, remarried, and asked her to live with them. How, sadly, it turned into a case where Jean's lying and stealing became intolerable; and, when confronted with it, how she ran away, and, finally, devised a scheme to pay him back. We are dealing here with a pathological liar. "Yes, ladies and gentlemen of the jury, you may find him guilty of being a negligent father, but he did not rape his daughter."

The prosecution then presented their case. The police detective confirmed Jean's allegations when she first pressed charges. A therapist (one I found who took Medicaid) testified that Jean's story had remained consistent and that she exhibited the symptoms of a sexually abused victim.

Then everyone sat riveted when prosecutor X called Jean to the stand. I hadn't seen her yet because she was sequestered in the County Attorney's Office. When the door in the back of the room opened, Jean just stood there and stared. There she was in her "lucky" outfit—dungarees, cotton shirt and beat-up windbreaker. She walked to the witness stand with her head down. When she took her seat, we locked eyes for a few seconds before she lowered them again when prosecutor X asked her name.

The whole time she testified, she spoke in the same manner she had always shown when speaking to me. There was no phony attempt to make a good impression. Her eyes remained downcast, she answered the questions slowly, softly, and flatly as prosecutor X led her step-by-step through her tormented background. *Is she reaching the jury on a credible, gut-wrenching level?* They had the saddest looking expressions I had ever seen on the faces of jurors. Jean maintained the same flat demeanor when the defense attorney cross-examined her. She answered his questions in as few words as possible sometimes barely rising above a mumble. She never seemed flustered. She never shed a tear as he gingerly, but methodically, portrayed her as a lost soul out for revenge for having been abandoned as a child.

When the prosecution rested its case, the defense began theirs.

An expert witness described the characteristics of a pathological liar, tailoring them to fit Jean's personality.

The defense attorney then called Jean's stepmother to the stand. Ann was a plain-looking woman who spoke in a weak voice. She vehemently denied she caught her husband raping Jean. She said her heart went out to Jean because she was such an unhappy, disturbed child. She insisted they tried everything to cure her of her pathological lying and stealing, to help her see how destructive it was; that they were patient beyond endurance. Finally, they were forced to give Jean an ultimatum: if she continued to lie, including lying about them to each other behind their backs, she would have to leave. They left $100 in their bureau drawer as a test. When it was gone, Jean denied she took it. That's when they told her she had to go back to the home for teenagers. She said that's when Jean stormed out in a huff calling her husband all kinds of names for sending her to an orphanage when she was six years old.

When prosecutor X cross-examined Ann, he proved that she had moved out the day after Jean said she walked in on them having sex. Would that have been the reaction of someone who alleges nothing sexual happened that night between Jean and her husband? Ann said that she just needed to get away from that whole scene for a while after they confronted Jean with stealing that $100. After some time away, she was ready to go back to her husband.

The jury was also riveted when they called Jean's father to the stand. He was short, husky, dressed in a navy suit, a light blue shirt and a royal blue tie. Even though he made a good appearance, he had a shifty look about him. He squirmed in his seat and his eyes darted all over the place. During both his examination and cross-examination, he maintained the demeanor of a distraught father. In variance with Jean, he displayed a variety of emotional reactions. Sad and guilt-ridden for having deserted her as a child; hopeful when Jean came to live with them; devastated when he realized she was a pathological liar; and horrified when she accused him of raping her. His voice choked up many times. *Does the jury see him as a father who tried to make up for his past mistakes and got burned in the process?*

Both sides had dynamite closing arguments—methodically building up their argument step by step. Now it was in the hands of the jurors.

I waited to hear the verdict with Jean in the County Attorney's Office, mostly in numbed silence—hour after hour—until the jury adjourned into the next day. When I got a child sexual abuse crisis call on my beeper, I reluctantly left, gave Jean my phone number and told her to call me as soon as she heard anything new. When my pager beeped, I quickly excused myself to a mother and child I was working with. It was Jean. She screamed into the phone.

"HE WAS FOUND GUILTY. GUILTY. GUILTY. GUILTY."

I was almost paralyzed, beyond speaking. "Wow!"

Jean was absolutely manic. I didn't even try to get a word in.

"I can't believe it. You should of seen his reaction when he heard *"GUILTY"*. He fell back in his chair and put his head down on the table. He was shakin'. He might of been cryin'. His lawyer was furious. He shouted out, "I don't believe it." Ann ran up and put her arms around him. She was sobbin'. Oh, you should of been there Millie. It was so wonderful. Everyone at the county attorney's office hugged me. The guards had to pull my father out of the chair to get him out of the courtroom. Just before he left, he turned around and stared at me. If looks could have killed, I would have been dead. I laughed in his face. Oh, it was so wonderful."

I let Jean go on until she was all talked out. Then I commended her on how hard she had worked over such a long period of time, never giving up, to get this guilty plea.

"The Jury believed you more than they believed your father."

"Yeah."

Then Jean stunned me.

"I'm movin' to Vermont now with a friend. My stuff is all packed and in her car. She has a house and she's gonna let me live with her. She is so good to me."

"When did this all happen?"

"A while ago. We waited until after the trial for me to go."

"Where did you meet her?"

"From someone at work. She was visiting her."

"How old is she?"

"Thirty-one years old."

I had an uneasy feeling but all I could do was hope that this would be a safe environment for her.

"Well, you sure are having one busy day. I hope this move works out well for you."

"I'm so happy, Millie. My father was found *guilty*. I have to say it over and over to believe it. I gotta go. Darlene is waiting for me in the car. Thanks for all you did."

"You're welcome. You did all the hard work. Good luck on your move."

"Thanks. See ya."

When my workday was over and the *Guilty* verdict had a chance to sink in, I flopped on my couch at home and just lay there, shaking my head.

I replayed the whole scenario in my head. I thought her father had admitted his guilt when he offered to plead guilty if Jean accepted a plea. Why would he have done that if Jean was a pathological liar and the rape had never happened? But why did he immediately revoke the plea after Jean had accepted it? Was it a clever ploy on the part of the defense attorney to disarm Jean?

Or did the defense attorney persuade Ann to testify for the defense once she realized that he was going to plead guilty and that he would forevermore be on the sexual offender list? Did Ann really walk in on Jean and her father but, in time, blame evil Jean more than her husband? In the end, did she choose to reconcile with him, without the stigma of a guilty verdict hanging over their heads? Was it all a clever scheme concocted by the defense attorney? Nothing but questions.

However, the jury wasn't privy to any of that above information. All they had to go on was Jean's word.

There was only one answer. The jurors believed that Jean was telling the truth and that her father and Ann were lying. The fact that he deserted her from ages six to seventeen might have also worked in her favor, attesting to her father's character.

When the county attorney, victim advocate and I discussed the case, they were elated at the verdict, considering the odds. They certainly had put hours of laborious work into bringing the case to trial. They said the defense attorney was livid—he didn't even think it was a close call. That he got a transcript of the trial and poured over every word to see if there was some legal point that would make an appeal possible but found none. Jean's father was found guilty by a jury of his peers and that was that.

Jean's father received the maximum prison sentence allowed by law.

29 It Happens to Boys Too

During my first years with Rape and Assault, I dealt almost exclusively with female victims of child sexual assault and accepted that as the norm. After child sexual abuse received national attention, I began to receive calls requesting information for male victims. Because there was scant information on the subject, when a caller requested that I interview three fourteen-year-old boys, I found myself in uncharted territory. Would interviewing boys be the same as interviewing girls?

TIMMY   DANNY   GERALD

The initial call came from a mother whose son, Timmy, had told her there was a neighborhood friend of theirs named Big Eddie who was acting weird around him and his friends. Timmy didn't want to see Big Eddie anymore. The mother said when she pumped Timmy for more information he clammed up and ran out of the house.

Big Eddie was married and had a family. He was well-liked and trusted in their middle-class neighborhood. He was home during the day while his wife worked. He had two hoops in his backyard in a black top area. The boys loved to go there to play pick-up basketball games with neighborhood kids and eat the junk food he offered. Sometimes he even ordered pizza.

The mother became suspicious and approached Timmy once again about it. Timmy reluctantly admitted that while he and two of his friends were in Big Eddie's rec room, there had been some touching he didn't like. Timmy said he was only telling her this because the two families were friends and he didn't want to be around Big Eddie anymore. He told her that was all there was to it and to stop bugging him. His mother suspected the touching might be sexual so she called Rape and Assault and asked if I would be willing to talk to Timmy.

My mind raced as she gave me this information. Would it be different to talk to a boy about sex?

I assured her that she had taken the right step in calling us and that I would be willing to talk to Timmy and any of his friends if they would come to our office. She could mention that I was someone who talked to lots of teenagers about uncomfortable touching. I recalled reading that young teen-aged boys are more at risk of being sexually assaulted by friendly authority figures such as a teacher, coach, youth leader or trusted family friend.

I was surprised when the mother called back a few hours later and said Timmy and two of his friends were willing to talk with me. Timmy said he would rather do that than talk to a policeman and possibly have his name get in the newspaper (an unfounded fear). We set up an appointment for them to come in.

The next morning, my nerves were on edge when I heard heavy footsteps coming up the stairs to our office. When I opened the door, I was relieved to see that the mother and boys had actually showed up. After we introduced ourselves, I settled them in our tight office space and told them that I would talk with each boy separately, just as we had discussed on the phone.

The boys looked like typical ninth-graders—lanky, dressed in t-shirts and shorts—too old to be kids, and too young to be mature adolescents. They were squirmy, giggling at each other's comments. I thought their behavior might be an effort to cover up nerves.

As I spoke to each boy in turn, I soon realized that even though the dynamics might prove to be different with boys, there was that same sense of urgency; these children longed to tell their story to someone they could trust.

As usual, I spent time breaking the ice with each one—telling them about myself and the work I did, and then learning about their families, interests, and school involvement. They seemed to be likeable kids and slowly opened up.

TIMMY

"Last Tuesday started out like many other days we spent with Big Eddie. We were in his rec room drinking pop and even sharing some sips of his beer thinking we were big shots. He was drinking more beer then usual that day and shocked us by giving each of us a couple of cans of our own. I knew I shouldn't have but I gulped them down anyway. I was stupid to do that. They went to my head. What happened was my own stupid fault."

"Timmy, perhaps you're blaming yourself somewhat unfairly. Becoming a teen is a confusing and vulnerable time. You're struggling to become independent but you're not yet aware of harmful situations that can make you vulnerable to abuse. There was a power disadvantage between you and Big Eddie—not just in terms of physical strength, but also in terms of psychological maturity. Try to be fair with yourself. Don't be too quick to blame yourself."

Timmy seemed to loosen up a bit, and I asked what happened next.

"Then Big Eddie said there were some pictures he wanted to show us. They were pictures of nude guys about our age who had a—a—hard on. We felt embarrassed and to tell the truth were shocked when he showed us the pictures. We began to laugh at the way the pictures looked. Big Eddie said it would help us become more mature to look at the pictures. 'Young guys need someone to teach them about those things.' It was true that the more we looked at the pictures, the more excited we became. Then he showed us some other pictures of girls our age in topless bikinis with hot tits and then we really got excited."

It took a long time to get this much out of Timmy and then communication broke down. He stopped speaking and wouldn't look at me.

I spoke calmly. "You couldn't help but get excited when he showed you those pictures. That's how guy's bodies are made, just like the hard-on the guys got in the pictures he showed you. It was Big Eddie's fault for showing them to you."

Timmy kept staring at the floor. I asked him what happened after that. He took a long time to answer as he started and stopped many times. He took some deep breaths and never looked at me.

"Then Big Eddie pulled down his pants and he had a huge hard on, like the guys in the pictures. He told us to do the same; it was all part of being a 'man'. We were embarrassed but we were so excited, we finally did it. Without any warning, Big Eddie grabbed my hands and yelled for me to rub his cock up and down FAST. He yelled out when he came as he rubbed my cock at the same time. I just couldn't stop myself—I had never felt so horny. Then he teased me by stopping and I begged for him to please go on. I yelled 'Christ' and begged him to keep doing it; it was driving me crazy. I yelled out like Big Eddie did when I felt myself coming— it was the greatest feeling I've ever had in my life. Then he rubbed Gerald's like mad and he came and he made a lot of noises. Big Eddie yelled for Danny to jerk off and then Danny frantically jerked off too. So we all ended up coming. It was like a game. It all happened so fast."

When Timmy finished telling me about the abuse, we were both spent. He had no way of knowing this was the strongest case I ever handled where the victims "cooperated" in the abuse and even screamed for it. I had had some girls tell me that tickling and rubbing the vaginal area felt good and even brought about orgasms in a few cases and how that made them feel dirty and guilty afterwards as though they had asked for it and even caused it to happen.

My number one priority at this point was to steer Timmy in the direction that was right for him. I chose my words carefully.

"Timmy, you have shown tremendous courage in coming here today and telling me what happened to you. Up until recently, if something like this happened to a boy your age, chances are he never would have talked about it; he would have kept it inside. He might have been left very confused, even questioning his own sexuality."

Timmy jerked his head up. "Yea. I wondered—you know—if maybe I liked doing it with guys more than girls. I haven't done that with a girl yet."

I was thankful for the little literature I had found on the subject. "Actually, young men are often assaulted by heterosexual men— Big Eddie is an example—a married man with kids—who also likes to mess around with young boys. This has nothing to do with you choosing to do this. It has only to do with Big Eddie. You aren't a homosexual just because you've been sexually abused. You can decide for yourself whether to choose women or men as sex partners when you grow up.

"It's normal for you to ask that question after such an experience. That's why it's important for you to talk over those feelings with a counselor. Before you leave here today, I'm going to give you and your mom the name of a wonderful male therapist who can help you sort this all out."

Tim nodded his head in agreement.

I moved the conversation forward. "My job right now is to guide you, Danny, and Gerald through this crisis state and, with your mom, help you decide where you want to go from here. Whatever step you choose to take, I will be there with you if that's what you want. How does that sound?"

"Good."

"I've now spoken to the three of you separately and heard your stories. If it's okay with you, I would like to meet with the three of you together and discuss what happened to you and what you want to do about it."

"Okay."

When the four of us re-assembled, they sat there stiffly, avoiding eye-contact. I told them that one of the hardest parts was over— they had each told their stories separately, in their own words, for the first time, and I had it on record. There were three corroborating testimonies. Because of their courage coming forward, they were now ready to process what happened, take action, and move on with their lives.

Their bodies started to relax—legs stretched out in front of them, arms became uncrossed, and eyes made fleeting contact. They all expressed a huge relief now that the story was out in the open.

Because they had willingly taken part, first and foremost, we had to address the fact that none of them thought they had been sexually abused. They were stunned to learn that because they were minors, Big Eddie had committed a crime—a felony—one that could send him to jail. They asked me to explain to them what was considered sexual abuse.

"There are many different kinds of sexual abuse. Because you are minors, what Big Eddie did was child sexual abuse because he got you aroused by showing you those pictures, had you touch his penis, and he touched your penis. As you know, sometimes the touch feels confusing or scary or even good. Big Eddie misused your trust and respect for adults. He got what he wanted without caring what you wanted. Your body is special and you should get to decide when you want to be touched.

"So remember—it wasn't your fault. Don't feel guilty because you didn't refuse right away. It's hard for kids to say no to older adults. Remember too how the touch feels good sometimes; how sometimes our bodies respond with pleasure even when we don't feel good about the touch. It can also be harder when you like the person and are caught off guard like you were with Big Eddie—sadly, good people can do bad things."

I allowed a long pause to let all this sink in.

I continued. "It would be helpful for me to know what happened right after the abuse was over and you were all sitting there with your pants down." After a slow start, words came sputtering out. Each comment invited more:

"We scrambled to pull up our pants. My hands were shaking hard."

"I was embarrassed after it was over. I felt dirty and weak."

"I felt so guilty, ashamed of what happened. I believed it must be my fault for letting it happen because it felt good, like I had done something wrong. I believed we were the only ones this ever happened to in our class."

"Would I have to talk about this in confession?"

"Let's not make a big deal out of it because it would just cause more trouble."

"Why didn't I fight back like a man at that creep? I was old enough to stop it."

"I hated Big Eddie for doing that to me. I never wanted to see his cock again. It was gross. Jesus—he was my father's age."

"Did the beers go to our heads?"

"What if we let him get away with it and then he did it to your kid brother later on?"

"But I couldn't get those pictures he showed us out of my head. I even wanted to see them again and come again. My wiener got another hard on sitting there afterwards. I kept trying to cover it up."

"I just wanted to go home, shut my bedroom door, and flop on my bed."

"I wanted to run out of there but I didn't want to be called chicken."

"We had always kidded around about playing with ourselves but nothing ever felt as hot as this."

"Does this make me one of those queers?"

"I wondered—would it ever feel this good if I did it with a girl?"

"I wanted to tell my mom or dad but I didn't know how."

I interjected that sometimes it's easier to tell someone you don't know, like me.

It took a long while, but I finally got the opportunity to ask about Big Eddie. What did he say and do after it was all over? The room became deathly quiet. Nobody wanted to speak first. Gerald spoke up first, and then others followed.

"He pulled up his pants, guzzled a few sips of his beer and acted as though we all just had a blast. But when no one laughed with him and just stared at him, he seemed to get a little nervous. 'Come on boys, we all just had a little fun. I bet you all loved it. It's what real men do. Next time will be even better. I have some movies that will make you come like you wouldn't believe. You're lucky—you're the only ones I would ever show them to.' "

"When we acted antsy, like we wanted to get out of there, he looked at us like—you know—like we were dead on the spot. His face had got one of the meanest looks I've ever seen."

"You guys better know that what happened stays here. You know damn well that I didn't force you to do a fucking thing — you all did it because you wanted it, even begged me not to stop. Is this something you want your parents and kids at school to know about? You just better sit on your asses and think about this."

Danny spoke up in a quivering voice. "I got real scared and thought I better shut up about the whole thing. Did he really have dirty movies that would make me come even more than I did? I started getting a hard on right then just thinking about it."

"I felt dirty and guilty and excited all at the same time. Was this something 'real men' did? Where else could I come like I just did? Why give it up? I almost wanted to see a dirty movie right then and there. Why not do it any time I wanted to? Who was I hurting and it felt so good. My prick was screaming for it to happen. I wanted to rub myself like crazy."

For awhile, it was almost as though the boys were talking among themselves, forgetting I was even there. As though they were reliving how powerful their erections and orgasms had been—beyond anything they had ever imagined.

Suddenly Timmy blurted out a comment that jolted them back to reality. "Remember what he threatened to do to us if we didn't come back? How he would get a ladder and climb into our bedroom windows in the middle of the night, that he could cut through any screen or glass and get in our bedroom when we were sleeping and stick his cock up our ass? Even though I locked my windows on those scorching hot nights, I still couldn't sleep. I kept thinking he was climbing that ladder. That's what made me say something to my mom."

Once they were convinced that their names wouldn't become public, they decided it was best to go to the police and tell them what happened. They agreed Big Eddie wouldn't be climbing any ladders once the police were on his tail. They loved the thought of getting back at Big Eddie and maybe even stopping him from doing the same thing to other boys. They were ready to take some action.

The day's work extended well into the night as I sat in on each boy's compelling testimony to the police detective. It was a weary group that grabbed my hands and finally said good-bye in the parking lot.

From that point on, the case took the usual course as I transitioned it into The System. For some reason, one difference sticks out in my memory, clear as a bell. When I would walk female victims from the parking lot to the police station, most girls gripped my hand tightly. The boys—I can still picture them vividly, under the lights—were in constant motion, fending off each other's nervous jabs.

The following days rolled into weeks as the detective conducted his investigation, Big Eddie got an attorney, the wheels of the criminal justice system took over, the boys entered therapy and I phased out my contact with them. They had taught me a lot. I moved on to another crisis call, another case.

The number of male victims coming forward continued to increase—they eventually accounted for about one-third of my calls during my last year with the agency. However, because boys were more reluctant to meet with me, I often had to rely on fragmented facts from distraught mothers. This forced me to change my tactics. I became a liaison between mothers and three top male therapists when I realized that boys often chose going to a male therapist over getting involved with the police. Since counselors were mandated to report any suspected child sexual abuse to the authorities, I knew that proper steps would be taken to safeguard the child. Kind, caring, professional help was what a young traumatized boy needed most. Because of my involvement in a multitude of cases, each one strikingly unique, I became well versed in the dynamics of male child sexual abuse.

I learned that there was a big difference in how teenaged boys and girls reacted to sexual abuse based on how their bodies physically reacted. When these boys got an erection, they often thought this made them a willing participant. These differences had to be addressed before they could surmount their guilt and shame and verbalize the details of the abuse.

I came to recognize child sexual abuse as a gender neutral violation. Its wounds are equally profound and strikingly similar in both sexes. However, male survivors are captives to a certain cultural bias that places a peculiar twist on their recovery. Our culture champions the image of the decisive, take-charge man. The guys get the message that they're invincible and that they'll always be in control if they're a "man". As a result, if a guy is sexually abused as a minor, he often denies or struggles with the reality of his victimization, seeing himself as unmanly or inadequate.

He often works hard at hiding his sexual abuse fearing rejection, scorn and ridicule. He often rails against his own innocence, shaming and berating himself for somehow "allowing" the abuse to happen. He often remains at war with himself—the harm done remaining active, the abuser's wound remaining unhealed.

The reality is that males victims of sexual abuse are doubly wounded—victims not only of sexual abuse, but of a culture with little tolerance for powerless males.

30   How Could I Have Forgotten?

My continued work with adult survivors thrust me into astounding territory. I discovered the incredible coping strategies the mind uses in order to survive when faced with incomprehensible or intolerable situations. It was a period of personal growth where I gained immense respect for these adult victims.

Over time, women started to talk to me about their "strange feelings." They claimed that weird thoughts and emotions made them wonder if they, too, might have been sexually abused as children, even though they remembered no such thing happening.

No matter how hard these women tried to ignore these disturbing feelings, panic attacks, and recurring nightmares, they couldn't. It was as though something inexplicable had overtaken them. Several wondered if they might be going somewhat crazy.

Once again, I was faced with a situation beyond my expertise. What *was* going on? What I did know, however, was that I couldn't just dismiss those unusual disclosures without first trying to understand them. So, in order to help me guide those women in the right direction, I tried to learn about this new phenomenon in the best way I knew how.

I listened to their stories.

LAUREN

Lauren was a warm, attractive, thirty-year-old, a college alumna, and a wife and mother of two pre-school-aged children. She had called me in response to the recent media coverage about the sexual abuse of children. Appalled by what she had learned, she felt the need to help. She had decided that educating young children to say no and to tell someone they trusted about any bad touching was the key to combating such abuse.

I was impressed with the research Lauren had done; she came equipped with information on several successful educational programs. She wanted to run the more successful ones by Rape and Assault and request our professional input.

I suggested she confer with our Director of Education. However, she wanted to spend time with me first because I worked directly with child sexual assault victims. She was eager to know what prompted children to disclose their abuse, how they expressed their memories, and what long-term side-effects they suffered.

I blocked out time for her because she was determined to protect children. Highly organized, she had zeroed in on a few educational programs that had proven successful in schools around the country. She planned to apply for a grant that would allow her to present such a program in New Hampshire schools. I applauded her self-motivated zeal.

As Lauren and I spent time discussing this project, she offered subtle hints that she was going through something personally upsetting. Although visibly shaken, she began telling me about a recurring dream. In the dream, she was in bed having sex with her husband when suddenly her father stood alongside their bed peering down on them. She always awoke from the dream in a state of anxiety. She said she had no bad memories of her devoted father.

Instinct told me I might be in fragile territory and should proceed with caution. I had read that repressed memories sometimes came in the form of dreams and thought that Lauren's dream could be a red flag. It might also provide a clue as to why she was so driven to help save young children from being sexually abused.

I focused on her dream—her reaction to it and how it affected her quality of life during the day. The more we explored that area, the more Lauren disclosed that the dream was disturbing and caused her to break down in tears. She said she didn't understand this scary thing that was happening to her.

I said her body might be trying to tell her something and one option would be to talk with a therapist. Lauren immediately started to cry and said, "Yes. That sounds like a good idea." We agreed that her crumbling emotional state was affecting her most important role as a wife and a mother and that she needed professional help.

I arranged for Lauren to meet with Paula, a clinical psychologist who specialized in the field. I was confident that Lauren was ready for such a step. When weeks went by without her calling me, I hoped that meant the two had bonded.

I had a close working relationship with Paula and we often shared information about mutual clients, if they had agreed to this. This vantage point gave me invaluable insight into the psychological dynamics behind individual cases, something that was especially helpful as I tried to guide clients in the right direction.

Paula told me that Lauren's presenting evidence pointed to the fact that she was a dissociative personality who had repressed memories of sexual abuse by her father that had happened when she was a very young child. However, because it was such a fragile area, Paula felt it would be destructive to "dig it all out" now. Such aggressive therapy could come at a high emotional cost, at a time in Lauren's life when she needed her energy to be the good wife and mother she longed to be. Paula said they would slowly work through Lauren's fragile emotions. In the meantime, Lauren's need to educate and protect young children would be a productive use of her time and would also enhance her self-esteem.

Lauren's case taught me that the pace at which possible repressed memories should be uncovered is best left in the hands of skilled therapists. In Lauren's case, many children were undoubtedly spared from being sexually abused because of her admirable, dedicated work.

FERN

Fern called Rape and Assault because she had heard about our work in the area of child sexual abuse. She was a volunteer at an out-of-state women's crisis center, working primarily with adult survivors. She thought we should meet, that perhaps we could learn from each other. So we set up an appointment for her to come to our office.

Fern steamrolled her way into our office. She immediately started talking about herself. I learned that she was in her fifties, an empty-nester, and was comfortably settled in a long-term marriage, with healthy outside pursuits. She seemed to lead a balanced life. I liked her.

She had a forceful personality with strong opinions on the role women's crisis centers should play in dealing with adult survivors. She had two years experience working in the field. Although she did not possess a professional degree, Fern offered ongoing counseling to these victims. While Fern was smart, driven, and dedicated, her uncompromising views left little room for discussion. I could sense she could be intimidating but through my work, I was confident in my beliefs and was not intimidated.

Fern bluntly stated that women's crisis centers such as ours should offer long term counseling to those victims. She claimed that her ongoing support greatly enhanced their psychological well-being. I was just as firm when stating that we at Rape and Assault were not trained counselors and that our goal was to put victims in the hands of skilled professionals. I said this approach also freed up valuable time for our understaffed agency to educate the public about the issue of child sexual abuse and to be outspoken advocates for how The System processed these cases. In the end, each of us held firmly to our set of beliefs and we agreed to disagree.

During the course of a follow-up meeting, Fern disclosed that she had repressed memories of sexual abuse at a very young age, by her father. These memories and the trauma associated with them had surfaced years later during therapy sessions.

What made Fern's case compelling was that when she confronted her father about this abuse, he was so overcome with guilt and remorse, he had tearfully confessed and begged her forgiveness. Fern said the validation was cathartic for her. Because of his admission, she eventually worked through most of her anger and had a slight change of heart. They now had an honest relationship with limited contact.

Fern was one of the fortunate ones. When most alleged offenders are faced with disclosures of repressed memories, they vehemently deny that there is any truth to the allegations. Furthermore, such disclosures often tear families apart and many family members wish nothing had been said. *What good did it do to bring all that muck up at this late date? Besides, how could anyone possibly forget anything so traumatic, claiming years later that memories had mysteriously popped up? Memories that had no doubt been goaded by a crackpot therapist.*

I struggled with my own nebulous views on the subject. I questioned whether repressed memories which surfaced later on in life were real. However, cases like Fern's supported my decision to keep an open mind, to judge each case on its own merit, and to keep learning as I went along.

My conversations with Fern also forced me to reassess Rape and Assault's commitment to do minimal counseling and refer victims to trained therapists. Our approach was supported when the New Hampshire Psychological Organization applauded our efforts by awarding me their 1990 Distinguished Contribution Award for outstanding public service in the field of mental health. This award confirmed that Rape and Assault was doing the right thing by passing along our clients to trained counselors, and I continued to partner with the leading therapists in the field. This was especially true when dealing with those perplexing cases of recovered memories.

MAUREEN

Maureen approached me at the conclusion of one of my public educational programs on child sexual abuse. Articulate, and dressed in a tasteful, casual style, she projected an appealing warmth. She was employed as a human resources executive for a high-tech company in Massachusetts. Part of her job dealt with sexual harassment in the work force and related issues. She was enthralled by the work we did at Rape and Assault. Wanting to pursue our discussion further, we set a date to meet again.

Over lunch, Maureen emphasized that she never accepted anything at face value. She needed all the facts before passing judgment. We shared common ground on this. Maureen did more listening than talking since she was interested in hearing about my work with sexually abused children and adult survivors.

Several months after our luncheon, Maureen called and asked if we could meet again to discuss a personal matter, which we did. This time, she projected a different demeanor. She was tense, nervous; her voice quivered. There was no small talk. She started right in telling me her story.

She said that a few weeks earlier, she had caught a graphic TV news clip about child sexual abuse. Without warning, she couldn't function. She had trouble breathing, her heart raced, her stomach cramped, and she barely made it to the bathroom to upchuck her dinner.

Stunned by her strong reaction, Maureen fumbled for a logical explanation. Reactions like that don't happen out of the blue. Because she felt emotionally wiped out for days afterwards, she searched for answers to explain what had happened to her. To help her in this quest, she contacted Dr. Shaun, a highly recommended clinical psychologist. Maureen figured that once she personally understood the cause and effect, she could deal with the situation and move on.

When she met with Dr. Shaun, Maureen told her exactly what had occurred and how she wanted the psychologist to level with her about what she was faced with. Upon hearing the details, Dr. Shaun said that Maureen's gut reaction to the TV news segment might have been triggered by a buried memory in her unconscious. On hearing this, Maureen let out a huge sigh of relief. That sounded pretty normal. We all have buried stuff lurking in our unconscious. That didn't make her "crazy." She could accept that explanation and move on with her life.

However, Dr. Shawn suggested that Maureen have a couple more sessions. Sometimes uncovering buried memories in such a dramatic fashion can trigger emotional repercussions that she might want to work through. That sounded reasonable enough, so Maureen agreed.

At their next session, Dr. Shawn suggested they start at any place that was comfortable for Maureen; that, together, they would ultimately get to where they had to go. Maureen uncharacteristically struggled for words as she tried to describe to me what happened next. She wasn't quite sure what *did* happen next. She remembered feeling dizzy, vulnerable, and somewhat like a sad, scared child. This was accompanied by an indescribable "strange head," as though something unfamiliar was going on in there against her will. She hated the feeling. She was used to being in control.

Then, out of nowhere, she found herself speaking in a childlike voice of a young kid who called himself Boy. In a defiant tone, Boy blurted out that Maureen's father had touched her in a bad way and that he was not a nice person. Then Boy said that his job was to take over when Maureen got too scared. When Dr. Shaun asked how old they were, he said they were four years old. Boy boasted about how well he did his job.

Then, as quickly as the boy had appeared, he was gone. Maureen was dumbfounded. Where did that voice come from? Why a *boy*? Her loving father *never* touched her in a bad way! She was incredulous. How could such a voice come out of her?

Maureen said it was such an unsettling experience, it left her drained; her shaking legs barely made it out to the car. She replayed the scene over and over in her mind as she drove home. However, later that day, when she remembered Boy's spunk when he spoke up in defense of the scared child, it put a skip in her step. She liked him. The whole experience was baffling and left her woozy and lightheaded for days afterwards.

As the memory of Boy lingered in her mind, she had an eerie feeling that she had met him before in her dreams. He was cute, likeable but mischievous. One such dream involved a sad, female child who was in danger, in the midst of a chaotic scene, and Boy ran and quickly unplugged the light and everything went black.

Later on that week when she was strolling through the aisles in *Macy's,* she spotted a cuddly stuffed animal—a golden-colored dog with floppy ears and a playful face. She sensed Boy begging for the dog. How ridiculous! She ignored the plea and concentrated on picking out a bathing suit for the summer. Two hours later, bathing suit in hand, she ambled through the crowded parking lot cuddling a big stuffed dog who took his rightful place on the passenger's seat.

Maureen said it was all too bizarre to talk about with family or friends. "Can you imagine the reaction of my colleagues if I told them I bought a big stuffed dog because the 'Boy' in me wanted it?" Although I didn't comment, the picture of this successful executive buying and cuddling a stuffed animal in public made *me* a little uncomfortable. Maureen went on to say that she felt safe talking to me—I must have heard everything in my line of work.

I told Maureen that I had minimal knowledge and experience in the field of repressed memories. I was just beginning to learn about it. That, quite honestly, I could probably learn more from her than she could from me. Luckily, she understood my limitations and appreciated my honesty. With that behind us, we eagerly entered into a conversation questioning whether or not we believed that such a phenomenon even existed. However, if it didn't, what else could account for her strong reaction to that TV news clip?

After our luncheon, she continued with her once-a-week therapy sessions determined to get to the bottom of this shocking intrusion into her life.

Dr. Shaun suggested they try hypnosis; this had proven successful in similar cases. She said hypnosis would be a state similar to the one she was in when Boy had spontaneously appeared. Although apprehensive and skeptical, Maureen agreed to give it a try.

She struggled for words as she tried to explain to me what it was like to go into a hypnotic trance. She said it was both easier and more difficult than she would have imagined. When Dr. Shaun had her lie on the couch and close her eyes, she softly recapped why Maureen had sought counseling and what she had just said on that particular day. Then she encouraged her to speak whenever she was ready.

That first time, she said she lay there as still as she could be and waited for something to happen. She felt restless, disoriented, trapped; she wanted to escape. She had nervous, nagging thoughts about how much this waste of time was costing her.

However, the longer she lay there in the stillness of her thoughts, the more she blocked out external stimuli, until a different state seemed to overtake her. Eventually—she couldn't say how it happened, only that it did—eventually, she found herself saying something.

That was the first of a series of ongoing trances that exhibited a similar pattern. Maureen said the trances usually began with apprehension, dizziness, and a "strange head." She said she never knew what to expect when she lay down on that couch and closed her eyes. Week after week, different voices came through, each one telling her/his personal story, in her/his unique way.

Maureen gained a sense that hypnosis was not some kind of voodoo that put her under Dr. Shaun's spell. To her, hypnosis simply tapped into her own ability to go into a deep state of concentration, blocking out outside stimuli and bypassing defenses that had been built up over a lifetime. At no time did she feel coerced into saying anything. She was always in charge of her thoughts; Dr. Shaun would begin each trance session with words like, "You know how to get where you need to go."

Maureen dreaded the trances—they didn't get easier with time; if anything, they got harder. Sometimes she had to stop because the room would start spinning around. She left the sessions physically and mentally exhausted, wiped out for days. Vertigo plagued her as she tried to regroup and function in her daily life. Her biggest relief came when she arrived at her session and Dr. Shaun said she thought it best that they take a break from trances—it was time to slow down and talk about what was going on in her daily life.

As the months dragged on, Maureen never doubted the profundity of her journey, one that she likened to a primal force that kept thrusting her forward.

The case fascinated me. At times it was like trying to put pieces of a jigsaw puzzle together in order to solve a mystery. I was often amazed that she could function in such a high-powered job while her psyche was being fractured into fragments.

Her home front applied the most outside pressure. Maureen said that, at first, her logical, engineer-minded husband was supportive. However, as time went on, he became leery of the process as Maureen became progressively immersed in what she was going through. He complained that her mind seemed "elsewhere" and that their marriage was playing "second fiddle." She tried to explain to him, with little success at first, that she was in the throes of something beyond her control and was desperately trying to figure it out. With time, they decided this was "her journey" and he respected the space she needed to take it privately. With this understanding, her love for him grew.

While I felt her self-absorption was understandable, I wondered if it might be taking a bigger emotional toll than she was ready to admit. Although I voiced that I wished she had others to turn to for support, she claimed the story was just too bizarre to share. How could she explain something she didn't understand herself? Furthermore, she couldn't destroy her successful persona and have people view her as a "crazy." It was taking all her strength just to hold herself together; she couldn't take on that added pressure. I could only empathize and support her courage as she traveled on her solitary journey. Maureen assured me that my listening to her and trying to understand was helpful.

As Maureen's "memories" continued to surface in the safe environment of therapy, Dr. Shaun concluded that Maureen had a dissociative disorder, a refined coping mechanism that had enabled Maureen to function on a high level because other personalities (alters) had kept her memories of being sexually abused by her father at a very young age buried in her unconscious.

Dr. Shaun proceeded at a slow, clinical pace. She diagnosed Maureen as having *Dissociative Identity Disorder (DID)*. *DID* was formerly called *Multiple Personality Disorder (MPD)*. Because *MPD* patients had received sensational media coverage via *Three Faces of Eve and Sybil*, the supposedly extreme form of *MPD* as portrayed in those films was the one that stuck in the public mind. Today, the diagnostic term *Multiple Personality Disorder* has been replaced with the more inclusive term, *Dissociative Identity Disorder*, as the former doesn't accurately portray its wide range—from low-functioning to high-functioning personalities.

Maureen explained that, in *DID*, the dissociated parts are formed when a very young child is faced with abuse that is too much for her/him to handle emotionally. So, in order to cope, the child's mind drifts off to a safer place while the body memories are stored with a "helping" personality, who keeps them buried in the unconscious.

She said that this coping mechanism can serve a young child well. However, once in place, it can affect individuals in different ways as they grow into adulthood. After *DID* is ingrained as a defense mechanism, it can become a learned behavior and new "personalities" can continue to be formed, as needed, during different stages of one's life. It works, so why not keep up with a good thing?

In Maureen's case, because she was able to develop a strong ego and go on to become a high-functioning adult, her dissociative parts were kept safely buried in her unconscious. Her *DID* was unseeable to the outside world. She never "lost time" or had another personality take over on a conscious level as portrayed in *The Three Faces of Eve or Sybil.*

Over time, Maureen and I tried to understand this phenomenon and relate to the different personalities that had continued to emerge during her lifetime. Some of it even began to make sense to us. We were astounded that the mind could be capable of such a clever defense mechanism. However, sometimes, when we found ourselves believing it, we would stop short and ask ourselves if the whole thing could be a figment of her imagination. No one questioned the validity of the *DID* diagnosis more than Maureen—the one who always needed cold, hard facts before she believed anything.

Maureen's revelations suggested that her father had her perform oral sex on him when she was approximately three to six years old. Her inner child's buried memories of the abuse came through in trances and dreams, along with conflicting emotions—tenderness (Daddy hugs me and says he loves me); feeling honored (Daddy says I'm his special girl); confusion

(Daddy's doing funny things); pleasure (Daddy's tickling my pee-pee feels good); distaste (Daddy's thing in my mouth tastes awful); and terror (Daddy's making scary noises).

Confronted with such evidence, along with the appropriate emotional responses, Maureen was able to sustain a belief in the process. However, because she never regained a single conscious memory of her father sexually abusing her, she couldn't accept it as 100% factual, even though she sensed it had happened. Because her parents were dead, it couldn't be validated.

I wondered if Maureen might be experiencing a collision of two powerful forces—a strong ego that had enabled her to lead a successful life and, therefore, continued to fight for its existence, along with a powerful unconscious that demanded expression. Even though her unconscious never seemed to throw more at her than she could handle, I questioned whether she might crack under the pressure. Yet, even though she said the therapeutic process left her dizzy, reeling, and physically drained, somehow, she persevered. Maybe she was used to being a survivor?

In the end, Maureen reluctantly had to concede that there are some things you just can't know. She said that the piece of the puzzle that finally put her journey to rest was when she was convinced that a very young child (under seven years old), who hasn't yet developed the ability to think abstractly and to make rational judgments about concrete or observable phenomenon, doesn't process information in the same, logical way that an older child or adult does. Therefore, the memories of such a young child won't return in the form of concrete evidence that the adult in her longs for. Maureen came to realize that she had to go into an altered state of consciousness, such as dreams or trances, to retrieve those memories, a primitive state more attuned to that of a young child.

For Maureen, those memories often surfaced in the form of spontaneous body memories both in and out of therapy—sexual arousal, tears, stomach aches, and nightmares. Those body memories heightened during dreams and trance states, similar to the state her child, herself, would have been in when she processed them. To Maureen, they were her "proof."

With rare exceptions, she didn't contact her therapist between sessions that averaged about forty a year. No drugs were ever used during the course of her therapy and she didn't take any prescription medications.

When Maureen terminated therapy four years later, she said she was a stronger person than when she started. During the therapeutic process, she integrated the dissociated parts of herself that she had been running away from. Integrating both her shadow side as well as the positive aspects of her personalities, gave her a self-understanding and inner peace she had not known before.

In many ways, Maureen said it had become a spiritual journey. Because her repressed child was so well protected and nurtured in her unconscious, Maureen felt that her inner child's ability to dissociate was a gift that had been given to her when she was too young to defend herself. This gift had enabled her to overcome the initial trauma and go on to lead a productive life as a college graduate, wife, mother, and business executive. However those successes hadn't negated her soul's demand that she face the truth about herself in order to become "whole," a yearning so powerful, it could not be denied.

As I listened to more of these stories and educated myself further on the field of dissociation, I accepted the possibility that there could be a process whereby a group of normally connected mental processes such as emotions and understanding could be separated from the rest of the mind—a defense mechanism against severe trauma.

My limited number of cases offered some credence to the school of thought that claimed that those separated memories remained in the body and, given the right set of circumstances, a person could react to them without having any idea why. That it might also be possible for those repressed memories to actually break through into consciousness later on in life.

However, I could also understand why this phenomenon quickly turned into a hotly debated issue about the reliability of those so-called recovered memories. There was just too much ambiguity surrounding the issue and too much room for "quacks" to distort the picture.

Lauren, Fern, and Maureen were examples of how dissociative disorders were possibly used as healthy coping mechanisms for young children, ones that enabled them to survive the trauma of child sexual abuse and go on to become high-functioning adults. Their cases also showed that, even though they had become high-functioning adults, they eventually faced pressure from an unyielding unconscious demanding expression. That those powerful forces had perhaps pushed each one into therapy, a safe environment where they finally integrated their fragmented selves and became whole entities.

As I became more aware of the varying degrees that dissociative disorders could present, I soon realized the limited role Rape and Assault could play in these cases. I had learned much from Lauren, Fern, and especially Maureen. However, because of the time limitations of my job, my focus had to be on educating myself about the topic, detecting potential cases, and then putting them in the hands of qualified professionals. Studies showed that long-term therapy of three to five times a week, for three to five years was the most successful. Even though, realistically, few could afford this luxury, it was preferable that they get as much therapy as they could afford, as warranted.

STUDIES ON DISSOCIATIVE IDENTITY DISORDER (DID)

One is not born with *DID*. It is a creative and life-saving adaptive strategy, not a sign of a mental illness.

DID usually develops before the age of seven. It is a gift that allows young children to deal with the pain of abuse by developing lifesaving defenses whereby they can mentally escape a situation they can't physically leave. The body and mind seem to separate. While the body is being hurt, the child no longer feels it because the mind manages to escape to a safe place.

Not everyone can become a dissociative. Those who could were luckier. Usually they are intelligent, creative, smart, resourceful, and more than anything else, survivors.

Dissociative parts are for the most part good friends. They have come to a child's rescue, endured her pain, and hid lots of her feelings when it wasn't safe to have those feelings and she couldn't find a safe person with whom to share them.

DID is a way of coping and channeling the hurt so the person can function and survive. It numbs the pain, but, unfortunately, the pain doesn't just dissolve. Eventually, the pain must be released so it can go away. This step has proven most successful when the dissociative parts are integrated in a safe, therapeutic setting.

Dissociatives are conformists—they are so far from being "mad", that some of the dissociative parts are like different types of normal people.

You can learn a lot about contemporary culture from the life of a dissociative.

Trance (hypnotic) states are one of the few common denominators in a majority of individuals who in the course of the past 200 years or so, have satisfied the DSM criteria for *DID*.

There is a body of evidence for and against the validity of Dissociative Identity Disorders. To this day, it remains a controversial topic.

In my limited experience with recovered memories, I never handled a case that I thought was prosecutable in a court of law, one that would pass the stiff test of being proved "beyond a reasonable doubt." Whenever I read media reports of such cases being prosecuted, I never felt there was enough hard-core evidence. They resulted in *Not-Guilty* verdicts, thereby sending out biased messages that such memories were probably produced by overzealous therapists and suggestible clients.

To me, at this point in time, prosecuting cases of recovered memories does more harm than good. It sets back the cause to educate a skeptical public to keep an open mind about the controversy. An alternative choice for alleged victims seeking retribution could be suing for damages in a civil trial, where the standard of proof is lower. However, this would entail hiring a lawyer and paying court fees, an expense few can afford.

Based on a 2010 article, *Questions and Answers about Memories of Childhood Abuse [www.aps.org/topics/memories.html]*, the existence of repressed memories remains a controversial topic in the field of psychology. Some studies have concluded such repressed memories can occur in victims of trauma, while others dispute it. According to the *American Psychological Association*, it is not currently possible to distinguish a true repressed memory from a false one without corroborating evidence.

Rape and Assault occasionally received crisis calls from individuals whose disorders were at the low end of the functionality continuum. They seemed to have no coherent center that enabled them to function on a conscious level. Some referred to themselves as multiple personalities who proceeded to tie up our crisis line. Bizarre stories, ritualistic abuse and even killings were reported, sometimes undocumented after a thorough police investigation. Although we treated every caller with respect and dignity, we had to recognize our limitations. For those repeat callers, our volunteers were given lists of their names and were trained to refer them to the mental health workers involved in their cases or give them referrals. New cases were referred to me for assessment.

31 Social Workers and Foster Parents

As stated previously, sometimes Rape and Assault was at odds with the Department of Children and Youth Services (DCYS). Many social workers said that, by law, we should call them rather than interviewing children, bringing them to the police station, and then sitting in on police investigations. Actually, after a child disclosed alleged sexual abuse to me, it was the parents' or the school's choice whether to call DCYS or the police. If parents chose to contact the police, then both the parents and the detective in charge usually asked me to support the terrified child when she told her story.

Rape and Assault felt that it made little difference who was called first because each agency was mandated to notify the other in every case of alleged child sexual abuse so it always ended up in The System—the ultimate goal.

Until a more collaborative approach was implemented for children alleging sexual abuse, Rape and Assault felt that we provided a service for those who were too scared to get involved with The System without first knowing what, if any, sexual abuse had occurred, and what would happen if they disclosed alleged abuse to the authorities. My job was to get the frightened child to tell her story. If sexual abuse was alleged, I explained the legal procedures to both the child and the parents and gently guided them into The System. We also eased their trauma by offering to support them throughout the lengthy legal process. Many parents said we were a lifeline in a time of crisis.

However, in spite of our differences, I never lost sight of DCYS' caring efforts to protect children at risk. Time and time again I saw social workers go beyond the call of duty to help suffering children, demonstrating to me how they are often overworked, underpaid, and underappreciated.

David Pelzer expresses similar views in his book, *A Child Named It: One Child's Courage to Survive*. David takes us into a world rarely seen by the general public as he tells his personal story through the eyes of a tortured, destined-to-fail child, who is "placed" into the care of others.

> As an adult survivor, I am forever grateful to "The System" that so many in society ridicule without mercy.
>
> My social worker stays etched in my mind simply because of her genuine concern for my safety and security. Very few people know what Child Protective Service workers go through.
>
> There are many who believe that social workers are merely home wreckers who barge into a private residence and pluck a child from the arms of a loving parent. Or that they never respond to a real case involving child abuse. There are of course those cases where this is sadly true, and they should be reported.
>
> There are too few social workers available to respond to the never-ending siege of "youth at risk." For them, a minor who is most in harm's way receives immediate attention. Once a report is under investigation, no information can be given to the general public on the status of the case, which causes stress to those who dared to file the report and who in turn may surmise that social services never follows through. Again, the operating principle of social services is to

preserve the privacy, safety and security of the minor.

Burnout plays a major role for these angels—whose sole purpose is that of saving the life of a child.

David Pelzer claims that foster parents are often misunderstood. Because only problem cases make the news, many people view foster parents in a negative light. The truth is that most foster parents take in confused, wounded children and give them lots of tender loving care. The shell-shocked looks of the damaged children I worked with who had to be taken out of their homes are etched in my mind. I was always grateful that there was someone to take care of them. David Peltzer echoes the thoughts of some foster children.

As for my foster parents, *they* made me the person I am today. *They* took in a heap of hideous mass and transformed a terrified child into a functional, responsible human being. I owe each of them so much.

I will never understand why *these* people put up with so much. One can barely fathom what it is like to deal with a child who came from a past like mine, let alone the half a dozen other foster children residing in the average foster home.

And yet, the general public rarely hears of the love and compassion for what some folks dub F-parents. They think that foster parents are only doing it for the money.

It appears that foster parents only receive attention when a child is hurt while under guardianship of foster care. The press clamors to "inform" the public of a child victim becoming victimized again. Because of such publicity, the question brought up by many is, has "The System" failed the child again? However, those cases are rare, and they undermine the incredible work that foster care performs. There are literally millions of children in need and only several thousands of homes available.

Like a great deal of those in foster care, I didn't know how good I had it until I moved out on my own. Foster children never forget their foster parents. Today my foster mother lives hours from my home. The highest compliment I can pay to my foster mother is this: she is my son's grandmother. That's how much foster care means to me.

We as a society are fortunate that there are social workers and foster parents who care for the neediest of children. After such a child trusted me enough to talk about her sexual abuse, in spite of her paralyzing fears, I was deeply grateful that there were compassionate human beings to protect and nurture her in her time of need.

32   Black Humor

Working in a twenty-four hour crisis center is synonymous with burnout.

One savior was our staff's sense of humor. At first, I was uncomfortable with it. "How can we laugh when we work with women suffering from blackened eyes and broken bones inflicted by angry husbands or boyfriends; or traumatized rape victims who fear strangulation; or innocent children forced to suck a penis? How can anything be funny in the midst of such pain?"

I eventually learned that we *had* to laugh. Once again, Deanna led the way. She had a fantastic sense of humor that we all benefited from. Sometimes we laughed so hard, I worried how we sounded to outsiders who might be in the building and perhaps couldn't relate to the constant stress we worked under.

We were great practical jokers. One time, I gave an all-day training session on child sexual abuse to crisis centers that hadn't tackled the issue yet. I thought the presentation had gone well. However, soon after, they sent me a blistering letter outlining my faults, the most serious being that I was homophobic. I was devastated and infuriated.

I called a female police officer who had attended the training session and was relieved when she praised my presentation. When I told her about the condemning letter, she said it was obvious that I had worked in the trenches and told it the way it was. However, she said many in the group didn't want to hear what I had to say, especially when I described some fathers' fears that sexual abuse by a male might cause their sons to become gay and how relieved those fathers were when I said that studies showed this wasn't so. She said the dissenters thought my words were a putdown on gays.

I scrutinized the videotape of the presentation. When I came to the homophobic part, the camera zoomed in on one disgusted attendee who sat with folded arms. She rolled her eyes to the person next to her who shook her head as if to say, "Can you believe it?" Completely oblivious to the reaction, I prattled right along. Looking back, I wished they had questioned me about it at the time. I would have answered that Rape and Assault's philosophy was that we had to respect all parents' fears, that it was not our role to be judgmental.

Deanna wrote a letter in my defense to the attendees, insisting on a face-to-face meeting. Because the air in the office was heavy and the student intern who typed up the letter thought we needed some humor, she snuck in a few off-color phrases as a joke. Then she put the letter on Deanna's desk for signing.

The intern chuckled as she waited at her desk to hear one of Deanna's famous howls. She waited. And waited. Finally, she peeked in Deanna's office. The letter wasn't there! Her scream pierced the office. "Where's the letter?" As it turned out, Deanna had trusted the intern's proven skills, had signed the letter without reading it, and Julie had already put it in the outside mailbox. The intern screamed hysterically about what she had done.

Pandemonium exploded. Julie and I ran outside and guarded the mail box in case the pick-up truck came. Sandy and Debbie ran to catch the mailman, in case he had picked it up. Deanna calmly called the post office and explained how we had mistakenly mailed a letter that could be devastating to a fragile client. They sympathized with our plight and sent their truck right over. Five anxious faces held their breath as the employee opened the box, and there was our letter right on top! All the way back to the office, we laughed ourselves silly with relief. The intern got more laughs out of that one than she wanted.

Another time, we feared possible retribution by the husband of a client. Deanna thought we needed some humor. After everyone had left for the weekend, she draped police "DO NOT CROSS" yellow tape all around the office. She planned to get to work early Monday morning and watch everyone's reaction as they came in. She would act nonchalant as we stood there in shock. Had somebody broken in? Planted a bomb? Stolen a client's records? She left for the weekend in glee thinking she had really outdone herself.

However, Debbie, our Co-Director, went to the office over the weekend to catch up on some work. When she saw the scene, she panicked. Deanna didn't answer her home phone. Terrified, Debbie called the Police Department. Police officers rushed over and did a Crime Scene Investigation (CSI). When Debbie finally reached Deanna and told her what happened, Deanna's scream on the other end of the phone could be heard by everyone in the office. We were lucky we had a good working relationship with the PD. They understood the pressure we worked under and knew we could be zany at times!

Rape and Assault shared office space with Hospice in a home owned by the hospital. Those extraordinary ladies shared a similar black humor. Every Christmas we had a Black Rape & Death Party and celebrated the joyful Christmas Spirit. We pulled that off because, in the midst of our laughter, we also respected each other's mission and knew how hard we worked to achieve our goals.

The Hospice Director admired my casual, professional-looking clothes; we had similar builds. I offered to will them to her if she promised to have me "go out" in a grand finale, with all the bells and whistles. She promised me the fanciest farewell that Hospice could offer and we gleefully shook hands on it. Every time I wore something new, she reminded me about our deal and told me to take good care of what I was wearing!

I had been introduced to Deanna when she was interviewed by Tom Brokaw on the *TODAY* show. One day I described my admiration for how calm and professional she was on TV, a motivating factor for my calling the agency to volunteer. She broke out in a hearty laugh, shook her head, and reminisced.

She said she had been too psyched to sleep in the hotel room the *TODAY* show had provided, in preparation for her early morning appearance. She finally got up at 2 a.m. then showered and dressed. However, she had left her make-up kit home! She couldn't possibly appear on camera without her "face"! She called the hotel desk and hysterically screamed her plight to the sleepy young man on duty. His skeptical voice implied that he couldn't possibly understand how make-up could be that important at 2 a.m. and said there was nothing he could do at that hour. Deanna mustered all her aggressive forces and demanded that he must do something—she was going on national television.

Finally, he looked up the nearest drug store that stayed open all night and offered to call and ask the clerk to call her back. When Deanna's phone rang, she said her new hero, the store clerk, had the patience of a saint as she rattled off her list of vital items— foundation cream; pressed powder in a shade for brunettes; a soft pink blush; brown eyebrow pencil, eye liner, and mascara; and a medium red lipstick—the long lasting kind. The pharmacist offered to tend the store while the clerk delivered the valuable merchandise. When the clerk arrived at her door, Deanna gave him a passionate embrace along with a generous tip. After she meticulously applied her professional look, she was now ready to face the nation.

The *TODAY* limo picked her up at 4 a.m. and drove her to the studio. She quickly glanced around as she was ushered into a small room and seated on a high chair. Before she knew what hit her, makeup removal cream was slathered all over her face, and then wiped off with a wet towel. After a cream foundation base, huge puffs of powder were swatted onto her face, forming a storm cloud around her head, before the make-up artists gave her *their* professional look.

That done, they seated her on a bench next to Harry Belafonte who was slated to be the next guest. He gave her a warm smile, flashing those famous white teeth. She was admiring his good looks when a crew member summoned him.

She waited alone, wishing she had a mirror to view her make-up. She wondered if the folks back home would detect her made-for TV make-up. Concentrating on her looks helped take her mind off her fear of going on live TV, not knowing what Brokaw was going to ask. She prayed that her knowledge and her new face would team up to project an image of a professional advocate for battered women.

No wonder Deanna had howled when I said I admired how calm and professional she came across as I watched her interview.

Laughter helped get us through each day. Things we ordinarily didn't find funny, we did. Laughter was as important as tears. Everything we joked about had a kernel of truth in it that could also have made us cry. There is a fine line between laughter and tears and we walked that tightrope every day.

33 Super Staff

With the sudden flush of child sexual abuse cases and its subsequent aftermath, I was amazed that our skeleton-crew kept afloat. I'd like to take this opportunity to thank all the fine, dedicated workers at Rape and Assault.

During this period, we only had six staff members: two Co-Directors, an Assistant Co-Director, a Supervisor of the Crisis Line, a part-time Child Sexual Abuse Coordinator, and a Shelter Manager, along with a student intern. Our salaries were pitiful; no one was in it for the bucks.

Although our valuable volunteers covered the bulk of the night and weekend shifts of our 24-hour crisis line, most had full-time jobs, so the lion's share of the work fell on the shoulders of the employees.

Because Rape and Assault was the only Women's Crisis Center in New Hampshire to provide hands-on advocacy for child sexual abuse victims, the state of New Hampshire turned to us for information and guidance. After Deanna testified before the highly publicized New Hampshire Senate Select Committee on Child Sexual Abuse, Rape and Assault received a framed recognition from the Senate honoring our work on behalf of sexually abused children.

Rape and Assault continued to break new ground. When they determined that education was the key to breaking the secrecy code surrounding child sexual abuse, Sandy, our energetic Co-Director, developed and presented Preventive Educational Programs for grades kindergarten through high school, programs that were eventually mandated in all Nashua, NH schools and several surrounding towns. These duties were in addition to her training workshops, writing grants, raising funds, speaking engagements, and balancing the books.

Sandy stayed with the agency until 1987 when she became the first Director of the newly created State Office of Victim Witness Assistance within the Attorney General's Office. That agency ensures that all victims of crime in New Hampshire are treated with the dignity and respect they deserve, and that the people who must deal with them recognize that the criminal justice system can be confusing and frightening to those who have been traumatized. In 2009, the Victim Witness Program of New Hampshire was chosen as one of two states to receive a Justice Department Grant, being cited as a model homicide services program. In 2010, Sandy was named an Inductee to the New Hampshire Coalition Hall of Fame.

Sandy's assistant, Debbie, helped ease the workload by gradually taking over some of the responsibilities. She was especially adept at public speaking, bringing much-needed relief to Sandy's ever-growing list of speaking requests. When Sandy left Rape and Assault, Debbie became an able Program Director.

As Supervisor of the Crisis Line, Julie's contribution was vital to the heart of our agency. She made sure the Crisis Line was covered twenty-four hours a day. Julie's diligence freed up time for Deanna to become the face of the agency, the spokesperson for needed reforms. My desk and Julie's were so close, we could shake hands. Each day, no matter what was happening in her own life, I could hear her give kind, unfailing support to battered women as she patiently informed them of their options.

Our Shelter Manager lived at our Shelter. She managed the demanding operations of running a successful Shelter—enforcing the rules, supporting the women and children who arrived in a shattered state, doing endless errands, and attending staff meetings—a job that led to early burnout as there was little private time. Because there was a high turnover rate, and because we had to choose a qualified candidate, this was a difficult position to fill.

Cecile came to us as an intern during her senior year of college. She attended our volunteer training program, manned the crisis line, and adeptly handled child sexual abuse cases. She eventually became our Educational Director, a polished speaker and public communicator. She held this position until she was appointed Director of Big Brothers/Big Sisters. Cecile put her career on hold to become a stay-at-home mom to three boys.

Deanna became my closest colleague. Because we eventually shared a multitude of duties surrounding the issues of child sexual assault, we spent endless hours together. She continued to be my role model. She gave fifteen years of fiery, passionate service to the agency, and forever changed the lives of women and children. I'm still benefiting from the lessons she taught me. She claims I also helped her grow, but I was the one who lucked out. Today, she is enjoying her well-earned retirement with her family, atop an Oregon mountain.

This small group of women activists was driven by their passion for the cause. They didn't give in to burnout. Each staff member became an important link of a unified team effort—women helping women. That passion rubbed off on me and my respect for them grew daily. I felt fortunate to be in their company, proud to represent their agency. We were members of a tight-knit group who valued each other's input. This rich camaraderie helped me grow into a more enlightened woman.

People often commented that our work at Rape and Assault had to be depressing, always dealing with life's seamy side. However, to me, those were uplifting years. When the Women's Movement knocked down the barriers of secrecy surrounding the abuse of women and children, Rape and Assault was positioned to take constructive action. We knew we could help those courageous victims who came to us for help, that their gutsy actions would profit others, and that we had the resources to fight for changes that would benefit women and children for generations to come.

I think the best way to sum up our special staff was when we had all gathered at a prestigious state award event where Deanna was up for recognition as a top state female leader. When it was announced that she had won the award and she headed for the podium, we cheered our lungs out as tears streamed down our faces. When she came back to the table with her trophy, we all hugged and kissed her. In the midst of all this, someone came over from the next table and spoke to Deanna. "Congratulations on a wonderful award. However, I want you to know that no award can ever equal what I saw—friends so genuinely thrilled for you. That is priceless."

34 Reflections

TWELFTH ANNIVERSARY   1992

For the fifth straight year, I spent the month of July in Maine at the Marie Joseph Spiritual Center, a mostly silent retreat on an isolated shore of the Atlantic Ocean. While there, I reflected on my twelve years working with Rape and Assault. Where had my consuming passion come from? I had never worked on a cause before. Why then? Why that one?

On reflection, what amazed me was how my life took on a new direction when I entered my fifties. Up until then, I had led a reasonably good life and had weathered a fair share of ups and downs. I wasn't restless or looking to make changes. Certainly not transforming ones.

The Women's Movement that began in the 1970's, when I was in my early forties, played a major role in my transformation. During that period, women became aware that they had a right to their own identity and collectively tell their stories. They began to make more conscious decisions about how to construct their lives, what their role in the family was, and how to balance the needs of others with the call of their own destinies.

Although the Women's Movement was the fastest growing social movement in the country, at first it had little impact on me. I was consumed with raising three teenagers during turbulent times. The women I watched on television screaming for their rights came across as pushy females who vented their collective anger toward men and blamed them for the state of their lives. I sloughed those women off and pursued my comfortable lifestyle.

In my defense, I could see why I was such a late bloomer to the women's cause. When I was growing up, attitudes toward women were drastically different from those of the young feminists. I had a lot of catching up to do. Sitting in my beach chair, lulled by the hypnotic sound of the waves, I thought about my life.

In 1939, I was twelve years old when the entire country went on hold to see if Rhett Butler's crass swear word, "Frankly, my dear, I don't give a *damn*," uttered to Scarlet, a *woman*, would get past the censors. When it did, it was front page news. By the time the feminists had turned twelve, they were blasé about vulgarity in movies.

I smiled to myself as I thought about how the feminists would have chuckled over what shocked me sexually, much the same way I felt about my mother's generation. Many in her era learned about sex on their wedding night.

When I was in high school in the 1940's, the romantic novel *Forever Amber* rocked the nation and was condemned for its blatant sexual references. Fourteen states banned it as pornography, citing ten descriptions of women undressing in front of men. But we women were hungry for sexy stories and it became the bestselling novel of the decade. I lapped it up. By the time the feminists entered high school, calling *Forever Amber* pornographic would have been a joke.

After I graduated from college in 1948, a pregnant sorority sister sought refuge in my New York City apartment to cope with this horrendous scandal. She spent fruitless hours in steaming hot baths, jabbing herself with a hanger. To hide her disgrace, she moved into a Manhattan home for unwed mothers which provided her with a fake mailing address. After her baby's birth, she beamed when she showed me pictures of her newborn and was heartbroken to put her baby up for adoption. She never got over it. Today, women have safer options that involve little shame.

When I reached my twenties and had married my college sweetheart, there were no newspapers, magazines, movies, or TV programs that raised women's consciousness. The media focused on such pressing women's issues as cooking, raising children, becoming a more fulfilled housewife, household hints to ease our workload, and the perennial *Ten Ways to Keep Your Husband Happy*. The raciest tip to make that list was farming out the kids for the night, putting on your sexiest negligee, and surprising your husband at the door with a martini when he came home from work.

As a newlywed, I moved to Connecticut and kept my job with *Ronald Press Company* in New York City, commuting with slews of men and a sprinkling of women friends. After a grueling year of long hours, I quit and took another job with *Marketing Research Company of America*, based in Connecticut. When I became pregnant a year later, I gave my notice; few pregnant women stayed in the work force. Luckily, the company allowed me to work on my marketing research projects at home. Even so, I refused their offer to continue working after giving birth. I decided that taking care of my family was going to be my fulltime job.

In my twenties, with three babies in three years, no throwaway diapers, a traveling husband, a tight budget, and no car, my days at home were full. I was wrapped up in my own little world. I loved being a wife and mother and had lots of friends; we visited each other and enjoyed fun outings. I had no reason to rebel and fight for women's rights.

When I reached my thirties and my youngest child entered first grade, I discovered that I relished my new-found freedom. However, after a year or so, I found myself itching to get back to work and I became a substitute teacher, the first of my married friends to work outside the home. I was able to be home when my children were and banked my income toward their college fund. Life was good.

Around this time, the nation's approach to sexuality was becoming more liberal. In 1959, D. L. Lawrence's book, *Lady Chatterley's Lover*, which had been banned in America since it was first published in Florence in 1928 because of its explicit sex scenes, was allowed in the country. I devoured the racy life of Lady Chatterley, whose erotic, game-keeper lover satisfied her unfulfilled desires. Although my own marriage was sexually fulfilling, this blatant way of expressing it was erotic.

When I reached my forties in the 1970's, the first tabloid talk show, *The Phil Donahue Show*, exploded onto daytime TV. I sat enthralled as he discussed hotly controversial topics and brazenly pioneered for women's rights. One show exposed the unspeakable for the first time ever on TV—Father/Daughter Incest. With live family members, their faces blacked out, he showed that incest crossed all walks of life, not only those who lived on the edge of society. I was stunned beyond belief. Although Donahue's top-rated show raised my consciousness, my friends weren't interested in hearing about his sordid exposures. I began to realize that I was going in a different direction although I wasn't quite sure what that was at the time.

As I hit middle-age and my children were leaving home to find their own way of life, the lyrics from *Fiddler on the Roof* spoke to me. *Sunrise. Sunset. Sunrise. Sunset. Swiftly flew the years. One season following another, laden with happiness and tears.*

When I reached my fifties, Dick and I were empty nesters and were enjoying our move to New Hampshire. The decade began with an unexpected series of powerful, evolving dreams that were to change my life. Like Dorothy in the *Wizard of Oz*, I was plopped into an unknown, bewildering world. After studying the meaning of dreams and doing research on my own, I realized that something extraordinary was happening to me. Looking into my unconscious mind had transformed my thinking and caused me to step out in a new direction. Gradually, the dreams became my guide and I applied the truths I learned to my waking life.

Curiosity led me to peek into the world of the women activists. On impulse, I volunteered for Rape and Assault Support Services (Rape and Assault). As I pondered that move, I wondered if the feminists' message had been seeping into my subconscious for quite awhile, prompting me to venture out of my warm, safe cocoon.

In 1980, it was still an act of courage for women to bare their souls; it was a slow process for women to find their voices. Because women were stereotyped to fit a certain mold, few abused women dared cry out for help. Even if they had, there was little aid available. Women kept secrets, fearing ridicule and shame. If wives were courageous enough to disclose abuse to their pastors, they were often told to remember their sacred marriage vows, to return to their husbands, and to try harder to make their marriage work. Marital problems were often inexplicably considered the women's fault.

The battered women who trickled in to Rape and Assault were among the first to seek help, and I suddenly found myself in the trenches with them. Many times I asked myself what in the world I was doing there. One thing compelled me to stick with it—those women of Rape and Assault were making a difference.

At first, when victims made me privy to the shocking details of their everyday lives, such unfiltered honesty, so raw and intimate, made me uncomfortable. Women did not discuss such things. I had barely gotten over one shock when another one hit me.

One day, a war bride with limited English couldn't find the words to describe her husband's abuse. So she unzipped her cotton housecoat, slipped it to the floor, and stood stark naked in our office to show me her bruises. Flustered, I quickly covered her up before Bob, our friendly mailman, could pop in with his cheery hello and usual chit-chat.

Another time, a woman from an ethnic background came in with a swollen eye. She feared for her life because of her husband's escalating abuse. Shaking, she whispered that in her culture, women didn't tattle to outsiders; she would be ostracized if caught. Although her eyes widened in amazement as we discussed her options for escape, she was too terrified to obtain a Restraining Order against her husband and went back to him.

A local physician who treated mostly affluent battered women told me they froze when he referred them to Rape and Assault; they were horrified that others in their town might find out about their secret. I told him our only option was to let them know they had choices and deserved a better life.

In time, I learned that we advocates had to be in a safe place emotionally before we could support fragile victims. As I tapped into my growing inner strength, I felt privileged to use it working on such a worthwhile cause. Because I also felt that a well-balanced life was key, I made time for my family, my social life, and my fun hobby of traveling on a tight budget. In my fifties, I was enjoying an early retirement.

Once again, destiny threw me another challenge. Now that battered women's and rape victims' voices were being heard, the climate became more conducive to disclosing other types of abuse, and Rape and Assault began to receive calls about child sexual abuse. Because I was one of the few volunteers who were free during the day, I offered to help Deanna in whatever way she saw fit. Under her supervision, I began a new career as an advocate for sexually abused children.

As I walked along the edge of the ocean's outgoing tide and gazed out at the horizon, I thought about how I was now being exposed to a naked view of mankind's dark side. I learned that innocent children were being sexually abused from infancy by fathers, relatives, teachers, coaches, neighbors, camp counselors, Boy Scout leaders, and clergy, among others. The impact of dealing with these cases put me on an emotional roller-coaster ride that, at times, took over my life. To be able to continue doing this work, I had to learn how to stay professionally detached so I could be strong enough to help mend those broken children.

After five years as a volunteer, I became a part-time staff member as Rape and Assault's Child Sexual Abuse Coordinator. Working for the only Women's Crisis Center within a wide area that advocated for child sexual abuse victims, I received calls from both victims and professionals throughout New England. When a leading newspaper ran a feature article about Rape and Assault's involvement with child sexual abuse victims, complete with pictures of Deanna and me at work, followed by a featured article on my work with victims, our calls mushroomed. We were the voices for those children.

Eventually, adult survivors of child sexual abuse contacted us. Early on, I was amazed at how many mothers of children I advocated for whispered about their own unresolved abuse in cases involving both family and non-family perpetrators. Soon other women who had kept silent for years came forward with deep, dark secrets, still harboring a crucial need to heal. This exposure taught us that the sudden onslaught of child sexual abuse cases wasn't something new; it had been going on for generations; it just hadn't been talked about.

As I reflected on my twelve years with Rape and Assault, I came to a better understanding of how I had transformed from a naïve volunteer to their Child Sexual Abuse Coordinator. Many contingencies had converged—my professional background, the Feminist Movement, the *Phil Donahue Show*, my move to New Hampshire, catching Deanna on the *Today* show, and working under the leading female advocate in the state. At times it was as though I had been swept away on a powerful tide.

At the same time that victims were enlightening me, my younger colleagues at Rape and Assault were also exposing me to the dynamic wing of a younger generation, females who were upfront about women's issues. Their candidness raised my consciousness. I was shocked by the subject matter as well as my colleagues' casual reactions to it. My peers wouldn't dream of debating such topics as the state of their marriages, how to attain sexual fulfillment, the pain surrounding divorce, and, especially, the role women must play in confronting our patriarchal society. Those feminists exemplified women working together with self-assurance and passion to be whoever they wanted to be.

Although my colleagues marveled at my independence, they noted my defensive stance against their suggestions that I become more assertive in certain areas. It was especially scary for me to allude to the slightest crack in my marriage. It was my rock. I gradually recognized that I didn't have to project an unrealistic, picture-perfect scenario, a cultural aspect of my times. I acknowledged Dick's ambivalence about my new role as a woman activist. They helped me understand that, when passion for my work sometimes took precedence, Dick could experience that as a personal loss. Such an upheaval in our lives called for major adjustments on both our parts, no easy task.

My colleagues continued to influence me and encouraged me to grow in ways I never would have otherwise. I became a stronger woman, a firm believer in empowerment. I realized that we women must help each other to achieve equality and balance in society. We had to redefine the idea of feminism to symbolize women coming together so they could lead fulfilling lives.

My personal transformation from a stereotyped woman to that of a feminist was a guarded one. I didn't slough off fifty-plus years of living under patriarchal rule overnight. It was especially hard for me to find fault with men. They treated me with respect, were fun to be with, and were interesting to talk to. I felt guilty when I said something unflattering about them. However, I knew the time had come to confront the patriarchal system we lived under, where men held power over women.

It was as though there was an old me and a new me. But it didn't have to be either/or. I could still keep the tried and true friends of my generation whose passions lay elsewhere. Similarly, becoming aware of batterers, rapists, and child molesters didn't mean that I had to think less of men in general. I could have a foot in both worlds. Reconciling the conflicting parts of myself made me feel whole and balanced, more comfortable in my own skin. During this period of transition, I continued to question many things I had always taken for granted. Why were women earning 72 cents to the dollar compared to men? Why were the doctors, lawyers, judges, detectives, and county attorneys I work with all men? Why was I the only female at professional meetings? Why should men dictate what women can and cannot do? I relished being a part of this new, vibrant generation which asked these questions and fought for much-needed changes.

As I breathed in the sea air of the Atlantic Ocean and felt my senses come to life, I wondered if I also fought for women and children in memory of those women of my parents' generation, including some in my own family, who couldn't fight for themselves given the times they lived in.

So, what was different about the 1980's Women's Movement that lured me into working with abused women, those same women I had distanced myself from so that I could project a winning persona?

For starters, I concluded that the timing was right. I had fulfilled many of my duties as a mother and had more time for myself. I had retired. I had moved to a new state that afforded me a fresh start. Those factors helped set the stage for what I now saw as the underlying release of my passion:

The difference in the Women's Movement of the 1980's was that the feminists didn't allow the victims to wallow in self-pity. They offered viable solutions, a way out. They helped victims take that first step toward healing.

That positive philosophy resonated with me, akin to my own life where I had established healthy boundaries that enabled me to move forward, find my own truths, and embrace life.

In 1980, the timing was right for me to fall into the arms of the Women's Movement. It was like a breath of fresh air. It supported women who embarked on that journey to make it on their own; it provided shelters for abused women to take refuge; it encouraged women to stand up for their rights; it supported rape victims; it exposed the reality of child sexual abuse, and fought for necessary changes in how The System handled those cases. The Women's Movement energized me because it gave me a positive scenario to work with.

I was energized when I realized what I was fighting for.

I was fighting for women in all walks of life.

I was fighting for myself to evolve as a woman.

I was fighting for women who were trapped in a generational cycle of domestic violence.

I was fighting for rape victims who were raped, not for sex, but as a violent means to gain control over a female, victims who often feared for their lives.

I was fighting for the innocent victims of child sexual abuse, to be a voice for those victims too young to speak for themselves.

I was fighting for adult survivors of child sexual abuse who had kept the abuse secret for generations and still suffered its consequences.

That was the call I answered when I was compelled to volunteer for Rape and Assault. Those women warriors of the 1970's and 1980's laid the groundwork that made my work possible, and I offered them my heartfelt gratitude.

Afterword

By the time I retired from my work at Rape and Assault in 1992, New Hampshire had become a recognized leader in serving victims of child sexual abuse. I am proud that our pioneering efforts helped change how these cases are handled.

There is no greater feeling than seeing someone else carry on your work. Recently I toured the Children's Advocacy Center of Nashua, New Hampshire, a forerunner of ten such centers in the state that now serve over 1600 abused children and family members per year. Bringing together professionals from law enforcement, social services, victim advocacy centers, and medical and mental health communities, these centers provide a safe setting for coordinating the investigative team. A trained professional conducts a videotaped interview while others view behind a one-way mirror, so the child is spared having to tell the story over and over. As I looked around at the soft pastel shades of the rooms, the comfortable parents' lounge, the victims' hand prints painted on the walls, and the inviting interviewing room, everything I had dreamed of was there before my eyes.

However, there is still work to be done. There will always be perpetrators lurking about. We must continue to make it safe for children to come forward at the first signs of abuse and then make sure they are put in the care of professionals. My interviews with hundreds of sexually abused children taught me that they *want* to tell their worst secrets.

I hope this book will shed light on what it's like to be a sexually abused child and what we can do to help them in their time of need.

Acknowledgements

Many people contributed to the writing of this book. To the following I offer my profound gratitude:

The women behind the feminist movement who laid the nationwide groundwork that made everything possible.

The original founders of Rape and Assault Support Services of Nashua, New Hampshire who had the foresight and passion to see the need for a crisis center for battered women and rape victims.

My colleagues at Rape and Assault who taught me that one person can make a difference: Kathy Schoenley, Jan Volante, Sandy Matheson, Julie Larson, Debbie Fauth, and Cecile Bonvoulier.

Deanna Crawford, Director of Victim Services of Rape and Assault, who led by example. She was my mentor, a treasured friend who nurtured my growth as an enlightened woman.

Compassionate therapists who mended the broken children I placed in their skilled hands, especially Dr. Ann Milgroom, Dr. Peggy Ward, and Dr. Ben Garber.

The Writers' Block, my weekly writing group, who convinced me that this story needed publishing and helped me craft it into the book it is today: Ellen Davison, Victoria Witt, Tae-hyok Kim, Phil Soletsky, Bettina Peyton, and Vera Clifford.

Judy Hannant, Cecile Bonvouloir, and Barbara Hagan who generously reviewed my manuscript.

Kylie Witt for her eagle-eye editing skills.

The sisters at the Marie Joseph Spiritual Center who enabled my writing to flourish in solitude and stillness, in the beauty of nature, and in the healing rhythm of the ocean.

My sisters, Doris Tudisca and Carol Treiber, who sensed when a caring phone call was needed.

My late husband, Dick, who kept my feet firmly planted on the ground and let me know loud and clear when the "tail was wagging the dog" or when I sorely needed a break.

My son-in-law, Mike Cline, who graciously welcomed me and my computer into his home.

My daughter, Pam, who pushed me to step out of my comfort zone by encouraging me to volunteer for Rape and Assault and then supported me every step of the way.

My daughter, Patti, who challenged me to stand up for myself and move beyond the stereotype of women in my generation.

My son, Richard, who enthusiastically accepted the formidable, technological challenge of putting my book on Amazon and E-Readers and transformed my loose pages into the finished product it is today.

My grandchildren, Genevieve, Haylie, and Cody who exemplified the trusting innocence of children, a fragile gift to be honored in each and every child.